DESTINY TALKS

The Ultimate Guide to Connecting to Your Purpose

JANICE GREGORY

WANDERING WORDS
M E D I A

Destiny Talks
The Ultimate Guide to
Connecting to Your Purpose

ISBN: 978-1-951029-21-0

Published by Wandering Words Media

WANDERING WORDS
M E D I A

For Jannie

To be your Mama—What a fabulous destiny!

DOWNLOAD THE
DESTINY TALKS JOURNAL FREE!

Thanks for buying my book! I would like to give you the
Destiny Talks Journal to go with it.

FOR THE FREE DOWNLOAD, GO TO

www.janicegregory.com/journal-download

CONTENTS

ITHAKA
Constantine Cavafy

As you set out for Ithaka
hope the voyage is a long one,
full of adventure, full of discovery.
Laistrygonians and Cyclops,
angry Poseidon—don't be afraid of them:
you'll never find things like that on your way
as long as you keep your thoughts raised high,
as long as a rare excitement
stirs your spirit and your body.
Laistrygonians and Cyclops,
wild Poseidon—you won't encounter them
unless you bring them along inside your soul,
unless your soul sets them up in front of you.

Hope the voyage is a long one.
May there be many a summer morning when,
with what pleasure, what joy,
you come into harbors seen for the first time;
may you stop at Phoenician trading stations
to buy fine things,
mother of pearl and coral, amber and ebony,
sensual perfume of every kind—
as many sensual perfumes as you can;
and may you visit many Egyptian cities
to gather stores of knowledge from their scholars.

Keep Ithaka always in your mind.
Arriving there is what you are destined for.
But do not hurry the journey at all.

Better if it lasts for years,
so you are old by the time you reach the island,
wealthy with all you have gained on the way,
not expecting Ithaka to make you rich.

Ithaka gave you the marvelous journey.
Without her you would not have set out.
She has nothing left to give you now.

And if you find her poor, Ithaka won't have fooled you.
Wise as you will have become, so full of experience,
you will have understood by then what these Ithakas mean.

I

YOUR SOUL WILL OUT

Joy, peace, and a life well-lived while creating a planet ever expanding with positive energy—this is your destiny, should you choose it.

If you long to create an amazing destiny, this is the book for you. *Destiny Talks* provides an overview of the tools that will lead you to your purpose. It will give you delightful paths to explore. You will uncover your core being, unbridle your voice, and claim your power.

The first step is to understand and cherish your soul. Then, unleash your spirit so that your voice and actions can express your soul and own your unique destiny.

What keeps us from our highest destiny? We lose ourselves to the demands of living. It starts early as we learn to survive at home, in school, in romantic relationships, at work, and, finally, as we manage the labyrinth of growing old.

So many people want us to be or do this or that. We may want to be this or do that for them.

Our parents may expect us to be successful, whatever this means to them.

Some parents want their children to be "A" students who go to prestigious schools and become recognized professionals, outstanding athletes, or famous stars. Others just want their kids to grow up, make a living, get married, and have children. Some parents may want their older children to care for the younger ones and, when old enough, make money to support the household. Many want their children to be just like them, to have the same experiences, easy or hard, that they have had, and to rise to challenges that they may or may not have met themselves. Sadly, some parents seem not to care at all about their children's well-being.

If asked, most parents would say they want their children to be happy. The problem is that they define their children's happiness in terms of their own values and experiences, rather than their children's. This may lead to *their* happiness, but does it lead to their children's?

This paints a grim picture of parents to those of us who were brought up in loving environments, but the tyranny of such parental expectations, whether spoken or not, can wreak havoc on our later lives.

Then there are our peers and romantic and sexual entanglements. Like Odysseus resisting the Sirens of Canosa, we need our mates to tie us to a masthead so we don't go astray. Here, too, is a sea of expectations fraught with unknown consequences. Our friends and loved ones, sooner or later, want us to be a certain way.

And then there are authority figures, teachers, coaches, bosses—the list goes on and on and on. So many people demand that we conform to their expectations, or else, what? Face loss and rejection?

It's a wonder that any of us become wonderfully happy human beings—yet it is our birthright to be authentically our unique selves and to revel in our gifts.

Make no mistake. This is not a book about blame. Without adversity, without boundaries, we would never know our mettle. *Destiny Talks* is about the joyful process of finding the diamonds and pearls that lie within us as we triumph over challenges.

Finding our voice, which constitutes our power, is an essential part of embracing our destiny. The voice is the human expression of the soul. It is sometimes expressed through living our purpose, but it is more eternal. You may have heard the truism that we are spiritual beings having human experiences, rather than humans having spiritual experiences. Our voice allows our spiritual being to speak out.

By voice, I mean both what we literally say and how our actions speak for us. Linked to the soul, our voices are powerful beyond imagining. The choice to remain silent or to speak out can change the course of history. What would our world be like if no one had challenged the injustices of the world, such as slavery, racism, genocide, and tyranny?

Like proverbial snowflakes, we are all matchless. What a mind-boggling thought this is! There are roughly eight billion people in the world, yet each of us, while we may share common emotions and thoughts, is profoundly unique.

If our planet and our spiritual and human essences are to evolve, all of us must let our souls speak.

But how do we do this? How do we claim our destiny? How do we get to know our essence and express our voice if it has been tamped down by years of conforming, years of running in the human rat race?

It is a journey, a wondrous journey, to Ithaka—if you will. It's the best trip ever! It's filled with adventures, twists, and turns which are yours alone and which you will triumph over.

There are at least three portals or gateways that can give you access to understanding your purpose:

- Your Lineage
- Metaphysical Tools
- Your Life Experiences

We will explore each of these.

We will travel to the islands of work and love where your destiny plays out. I will give you navigational tools such as The Passion Test and creative visualization to use in guiding your journey. Undoubtedly, hurricanes and sharks will assault your ship. Not to fear. You will learn how to weather the storm and banish scary creatures.

I refer to dozens of spiritual leaders and books in *Destiny Talks*. They are listed in the bibliography and at www.janicegregory.com. The list is by no means comprehensive but consists of authors and practitioners I have vetted.

MY UNFOLDING DESTINY

I am a fellow traveler. I spent the first two-thirds of my life arduously conforming. I earned two degrees from Harvard University. The first was a Bachelor of Arts with a concentration in English literature from the college, and the second was a master's degree in public administration from Harvard's

Kennedy School. I worked as a management consultant, primarily in small business development, for the University System of New Hampshire. I was married and raised one daughter and two stepsons in rural New Hampshire before moving to Newburyport, Massachusetts, and embarking on a whole new, astonishing life. My story is woven throughout this book.

Despite these conventional achievements, I spent most of my early life wandering in the wilderness, not knowing that I had embarked on my journey. At age forty-one, I was isolated, stressed out, and weighed down with responsibility. I was living in a dark cape house bordering the woods and a state highway in northern New Hampshire. My marriage was falling apart. Funds were short, and I bore the lion's share of caring for a newborn baby girl and two troubled teenage stepsons. At the time, I was also commuting to a demanding, unrewarding job.

My life was bleak. However, if I had seen any hope of happiness on the horizon, I would never have left my home to seek a new destiny. I have honed persevering into a fine art. Once I set my mind on a goal, I will work with single-minded determination to attain it. Hard work—that's how I became one of roughly 250 young women to gain admittance to Harvard in 1968, before most of the Ivy League colleges had opened their doors to women. Even Harvard only admitted one girl for every four boys. I studied relentlessly, foregoing sleep, dating, and fun to gain the requisite grades.

I applied the same principle of nose-to-the-grindstone to make my marriage and work life successful for twenty and twenty-five years respectively. But I couldn't do it. I couldn't control people and circumstances to make everything work out according to my vision. The forces of nature and fate were too strong. I was swimming against a current that would have drowned me if I hadn't changed courses.

Thank goodness, I did. My awakening came late, but I'm so grateful to know the joy of living in alliance with my soul and spirit.

Oddly enough, my journey began with a visit to a channeler, a man who lets spirits and guides speak through him. It was my first foray into the occult.

The channeler said that I'd spent the first half of my life meeting other people's goals without knowing anything about myself and that I would spend the next half discovering what I was about.

I dismissed him as touchy-feely, unhelpful. I just wanted to know what job to take, how to care for my children, and what to do about my soul-crushing marriage. *Come on now*, I thought, *what are the answers?*

But here I am, well into that second half of my life. I have encountered challenging adventures, to be sure. However, my journey has been filled with extraordinary travels, happiness, and love. Because it is an internal journey, there is no final destination to reach and then wonder if this is all there is. There is always more because we are each a boundless source of wealth.

Our journey, as you'll learn, is guided by our passions. So it is a happy journey, and the benefits of happiness are well documented: success, love, and abundance. The extensive research of Shawn Achor, the world-renowned expert on happiness, demonstrates how joy creates success in all areas of our lives. Reaching a goal doesn't necessarily guarantee happiness, but if we're on a joy-filled journey, happiness is assured. Seeing our dreams come true is just icing on the cake.

You only have to look at the burgeoning spirituality field to know what I say is true. Oprah Winfrey, Deepak Chopra,

Eckhart Tolle, and countless others have chosen a spiritual path of discovery and are enjoying long, enriching careers. This is not to say that the journey will always be easy. Your faith and courage may be sorely tested. But there are tools, which I will share with you, to minimize the risks and guide you in overcoming challenges.

TAKE YOUR MATES WITH YOU

A profound joy lies in deeply connecting with others as you wander through this earthly existence. This book provides the perfect vehicle to spark conversations. You might form a Destiny Circle with three or more interested fellow travelers.

At www.janicegregory.com/journal-download, you can download a free journal, which consists of the prompts at the end of the *Destiny Talks'* chapters. These prompts will aid you in self-discovery and thinking more deeply about your destiny.

You can also purchase *Find Your Purpose: The Destiny Talks Workbook* at Amazon.com. It contains all the journal prompts at the end of the chapters as well as additional prompts, self-discovery exercises, affirmations, and meditations.

Destiny Circle members can use the journal, the workbook, or a notebook of their choosing to create personal destiny profiles of their souls' essence. You can also use the journal or workbook on your own or with a soul partner to record your discoveries.

I recommend that your Destiny Circle meet once a week for 60 to 90 minutes to discuss each of the topics. I like to spend at least two meetings on each subject. At the first meeting, members discuss what they know about the topic and where members can find more information to aid in their quest. At the subsequent meeting, three or more members spend twenty minutes each sharing what they have found out about themselves. Other members listen attentively and provide positive insights.

Alternatively, you could hold longer meetings, once a month. You can also take weeks off to undertake self-discovery exercises on your own or with Circle members. The choice for how long and how often you schedule your meetings depends on your members' preferences.

There is no set curriculum for the Destiny Circle. You can tackle as few or as many topics from *Destiny Talks* as your members choose.

Like many book clubs, a Destiny Circle can have a social aspect where members catch up over coffee and snacks. How wonderful it will be to learn more about the soul mates in your circle.

Regardless of whether or not you form a Destiny Circle, you are going to realize happiness, success, love, and abundance on your personal journey to Ithaka. As soon as you step aboard your ship—and, by doing so, make a commitment to honoring your soul's destiny—you will begin to know ever-increasing and never-ending rewards.

Don't waste a moment. As the great motivational speaker, Wayne Dyer, urged, "Don't let your song die in you." Begin your quest now. Your destiny awaits.

II

The Journey

Traveling to Ithaka in Your Style

The twenty-two Major Arcana cards of a typical tarot card deck showcase the most important moments of life's journey. The very first Major Arcana card in the Rider-Waite tarot deck is called "The Fool." It depicts an innocent young man, happily journeying off with his pack slung over his shoulder and gazing up into the sky. He is oblivious to the cliff that he could plunge from if he takes one more thoughtless step in the same direction. His journey in the tarot deck will take him through archetypal challenges such as death, grief, poverty, and war, and through joyful experiences including love, friendship, children, and celebration, much like Odysseus's journey back to Ithaka takes him through the dark and the light.

We are all on this journey. How we give voice to our soul and spirit through our words and actions determines the unique character of our journey—our destiny, if you will. Our own reactions to life's challenges and joys determine the meaning of our lives. Combined with others' life choices, they shape planet Earth's destiny.

Seen in this light, our decisions, as we create our destiny, are immensely important. They can help lift humanity up or they can drag it down.

Our spiritual nature is innately positive. If our voice is negative, it is because, as the spiritual text, *A Course in Miracles*, explains, we are crying out for love. The only way to turn our voice from a negative to a positive force is to first understand it and then to consciously choose the positive.

There is no good to be served by our suffering. We cannot make anyone else's life easier, and, indeed, we will only add to the concern of our loved ones if we choose to live in pain. So, to the extent that we can manage to lift up our spirits, despite the hand fate deals us, that is the degree to which we enhance the lives of our friends, family, and mankind.

THE PROCESS

Where do we begin and where do we end our journey in creating a positive destiny? Our life's journey began the moment we were born. The starting line of consciously directing our journey is another matter. We could be anywhere in our travels, depending on how long we've asked questions about our life's course and sought to know and express our soul.

As a child, I envied those who knew exactly what they wanted to be when they grew up. At one point, I found the burden of figuring out what I was meant to do too difficult and decided that I would dedicate my life to a future husband's career goals. This was before the second wave of feminism in the '60s. In fact, much of my life has been spent trying to be the wind behind someone else's sail. Writing this book about finding one's destiny is a testament to how my cop-out has failed. I need to express my own soul's desire.

I've chosen the metaphors of a journey, *The Odyssey*, and the life cycle depicted in the tarot cards to describe the evolving process of knowing one's soul. Fortunately, our souls have infinite depth and riches to reveal to us. When we reach one destination, there is always another, more beautiful land to discover with its own cache of gems.

Another way to describe the process is that of putting together a jigsaw puzzle with more than 1,000 pieces. One feels great exhilaration on finding a small piece that fits perfectly into an undifferentiated landscape that is difficult to decipher. The difference in the real-life process is that we don't have the jigsaw box top with the completed picture to guide us—nor is our puzzle ever quite complete. Regardless, our soul's picture is more beautiful than any artist's rendition.

If we don't have the box top picture to guide us, how do we know where to put the jigsaw puzzle pieces? *Let happiness be your purpose and joy your guide.* You know that you've discovered a piece of your puzzle when a smile bubbles up from inside of you.

The Dalai Lama believes that "the very purpose of our life is to seek happiness." Both Desmond Tutu and he have suffered years of exile and oppression, yet they exude almost childlike happiness. In their book, *The Book of Joy*, they describe the eight pillars of joy: perspective, humility, humor, acceptance, forgiveness, gratitude, compassion, and generosity.

Janet Bray Attwood and Chris Attwood have developed a process for discovering your passions and using them as a GPS to find your life purpose. In their book, *The Passion Test: The Effortless Path to Discovering Your Life Purpose*, they ask readers to answer the question, "When my life is ideal, I am…" Then, the authors show how to reduce the number of passions to the top five and create a life to realize those passions and find extraordinary happiness.

Elizabeth Gilbert, author of *Big Magic*, talks about the importance of our curiosity and interests in guiding our soul's journey. She posits that not everyone has white-hot passions that they easily recognize. Rather she explains the importance of being like a bumblebee that cross-pollinates flowers by following our interests as their fragrances beguile us.

In addition to letting your joy, passions, and interests guide your journey, there are at least three major portals or entryways to understanding your soul and destiny: 1) delving into your lineage, 2) using metaphysical tools to make the unknown known, and 3) analyzing your life experiences. We will explore each of these portals in upcoming chapters as well as how to mitigate risks and manage fear as you travel.

After I separated from my husband in 2006, I started to explore my passions in earnest. I didn't exactly know, or acknowledge, what my passions were. The first portal I entered was filled with metaphysical studies—learning about intuition, astrology, and numerology. Both my father, a scientist, and my husband, a lawyer, had disparaged these fields, but I was free now, and I reveled in the occult. I attended spiritual retreats and sought readings from psychics, astrologers, mediums, numerologists, and whoever else I thought could provide insights into who I was. All the while, I marveled that my interest in the esoteric never waned. Instead, it led me to the portals of understanding my lineage and analyzing my life experiences to gain self-knowledge.

Destiny is a journey that goes backward and forward. T.S. Eliot famously said that "time past and time future are both contained in time present." How you interpret your past will shape your present, and thus, your future. The first part of this book views the journey from delving into your past, and the second part looks at shaping the future.

This is your journey. You can decide which portals to go through, which lands to explore, and what navigational tools will guide your travels. Your choices and findings will shape your matchless destiny.

DESTINY LANGUAGE

Throughout *Destiny Talks*, I use terms such as destiny, dharma, fate, free will, and karma. You will find a glossary at the end of the book which explains the meaning of these words.

CREATING YOUR DESTINY PROFILE
DESTINY TALKS JOURNAL PROMPTS

Prompts at the end of each chapter will assist you in gaining a greater understanding of your soul, your spirit, and your destiny. As you consider these prompts and answer the questions, a picture of your glorious essence will emerge. This is your destiny profile.

As mentioned previously, you can download a free journal with the destiny profile prompts at www.janicegregory.com/journal-download or buy *Find Your*

Purpose: The Destiny Talks Workbook at Amazon.com. The workbook includes additional prompts, self-discovery exercises, affirmations, and meditations. You can record your answers and explore your thoughts in the journal, the workbook, or in a notebook of your choosing.

Once you have finished *Destiny Talks*, you can review your journal or workbook entries to see how much you have learned about yourself. You can then build your destiny on a rock-solid foundation of self-knowledge.

Let's begin with your journey. You might start your profile by free writing for ten to fifteen minutes on what you know for sure about yourself so far and what you look forward to exploring in the future. Free writing is writing continuously without lifting your pen or stopping to edit what you have written. It's a great way to access your subconscious thoughts.

You could also free write your answers to any or all of the following questions. Choose whatever intuitively appeals to you. Skip what doesn't.

1. *Destiny Talks* begins with the poem, *Ithaka*, by Constantine Cavafy. What does this poem mean to you? If it didn't resonate with you, note that in your journal.

2. Where are you in the process of self-discovery? What is driving you forward?

3. What life obstacles have you overcome? What are the personal strengths and skills that have enabled your success?

III

Portal I to the Soul Your Lineage

About a year ago, I was querying my astrologist, Allice Haidden, as to why I wasn't motivated, like my colleagues, to help vast numbers of people. I felt abashed that I was consumed by a passion for the arcane details of my great aunt's life among the American and British literati in the early 20th century.

All the spiritual literature I love was urging me to be of service and to think *big*. Meanwhile, I sat on my sea-green couch reading dusty, out-of-print books that came to me from booksellers in the U.K., Denmark, and Kenya. I had nothing inspirational to say to hordes of people, nor did I want to save the world. I couldn't even muster enthusiasm to seek out coaching clients.

Allice said to me in her disarming way, "That's because you're involved in something greater: lineage healing. Your work is healing both those who have gone before you and those who will come after you."

I sat up and took note.

There's a body of research that says that when you heal yourself, you heal those around you. Many metaphysicians believe that you can help those who have passed on, as well.

If you clear a destructive family pattern, your children and their children will be freed from its harm forever.

This makes intuitive sense if you consider that our beliefs and modus operandi are instilled in us at an early age. We learn from our parents how to parent. One of the most distressing statistics is that the vast majority of parents who abuse their children were abused by their parents.

If our parents have a destructive, negative set of behavior patterns, it will take a strong conscious effort not to adopt these. I can see my siblings saying things to their children that my parents said to them. It's much harder for me to recognize things that I say that could have sprung directly from my parents' lips.

If we consciously seek to understand familial patterns and then decide not to act in the way we learned from our parents, it stands to reason that our children will not have our negative examples to follow in their own lives. Conversely, we can also see the positive and decide to amplify it for generations to come.

I looked for the patterns in my great aunt's and extended family's lives that were reverberating in mine. Not surprisingly, I found both the good and the bad. The good is how we strive to be responsible, sensitive friends and family members and to contribute to the greater good. The bad is how the women in my family often mute our voices and become immobilized by self-doubt.

"These People Choose Us"

I recently spent a delightful, soggy day touring Dublin with the Irish author, Patrick Quigley. He has written books on Countess Markievicz, a founding member of the Irish Citizen Army, a soldier in the Irish uprising of 1916, the first woman to be elected to the British parliament, and one of the first women in the world to hold a cabinet position. He has also written about the countess's sister, Eva Gore-Booth, an ardent feminist, poet, and labor activist.

Why, I wondered, was Quigley drawn to these historical figures? His answer was simply, "These people choose us."

They do.

We can only guess at the reasons why. Perhaps it is to heal our soul group (family and friends) and us. Maybe they have an important message for the world at large—a story that wants out. Our duty is to communicate their story. Often we feel like we have no choice but to tell their stories; we are driven by it.

These people don't have to be historical figures. They may be people we knew in childhood who have passed on, such as a grandparent or older mentor.

My fascination with my great aunt was born out of a two-week meeting with her when I was five years old. It tracked me down fifty years later.

After my divorce was finalized, I decided to take a new last name, rather than retake my maiden name, to mark the beginning of my new life. I believed in numerology's influence and struggled to find a name whose underlying numbers would give me the energy I sought.

(Numerology is the study of the symbolic meaning of numbers and letters as they apply to your character and life events. I will explain its tenets and how to calculate and interpret the numbers underlying your name and birth date in Chapter V.)

I tried out one name after another and jettisoned each for various reasons.

Saying I was partial toward taking a family name, I discussed my choices with a friend. We ticked through the choices, landing on "Gregory," my grandmother's maiden name. I liked the name Gregory because the Gregorys were writers and humanitarians. Also paired with the name Janice, my life path became 11/2, the master number of a spiritual guide, and my soul number became 33, the master number for healers and people who are family-oriented, responsible, and love beauty and art. The numbers matched those in my original birth name and spoke to me. Perfect.

Little did I know that I would soon begin channeling my great aunt Alyse Gregory's energy and I would start a journey to find her story on both sides of the Atlantic.

At age five, I met Aunt Alyse when we were both staying at my grandmother's (Alyse's sister's) house. My mother was in the hospital, delivering my baby sister, and my father, a physician, was off in Korea helping with the war effort. Aunt Alyse was visiting from abroad.

Coming from a large family where children were generally expected to be seen but not heard, I was enthralled by my great aunt, who focused her attention solely on me. Aunt Alyse sang me "Oh Susannah," taught me The Itsy-Bitsy Spider, and took me on walks where she pointed out skunk cabbage and other plants with strange names.

Aunt Alyse was seventy-three at the time. At age fifteen, she had traversed the Atlantic with a family friend to be trained as an opera singer in France. Even though her voice had been compared to Nellie Melba's, the famous Australian opera singer, she ultimately abandoned her singing career due to her fear of performing in public. She became a suffragette leader and eventually, even though she had only a high school education, she became the first female managing editor of *The Dial*.

The Dial, arguably the preeminent literary magazine of the 20th century (and perhaps any century), introduced modern literature and art to the United States. Aunt Alyse, at its center, interacted with such luminaries as W.B. Yeats, T.S. Eliot, E.E. Cummings, Ernest Hemingway, Ezra Pound, George Bernard Shaw, and Marianne Moore, to name a few.

One of the mysteries of her life choices, however, was that at the height of her career, at age forty-three, she left New York's literary scene, a life she loved, to marry and follow her husband's predilections in the desolate British countryside.

For most of my life, I knew none of this. To me, Alyse Gregory was just a wonderful elderly woman who had enchanted me as a child. I was always curious about her life but never met her again. My great aunt died by suicide in 1967 in Devon, England, when I was seventeen and living in Connecticut.

My research into Aunt Alyse's life has inspired me to explore my love of literature and the many ways she and I have both subjugated our voices to familial and societal norms. It has also revealed to me how important friendship is to creating a great destiny.

Finding the Wisdom

If you don't presently feel chosen, how do you find ancestral or historical mentors? I'm afraid there's no exact science to it.

Look at the people in your circle, living or dead, whose stories intrigue you and compel you to find out more. The patterns and choices in their lives hold golden nuggets of wisdom that pertain to why you are here on this earth. They have chosen *you.*

The nudge often first comes in small, unexpected ways that gather substance and momentum over time, like the snowball you roll to form the base of a snowman. Mine came over Thanksgiving dinner in 2010 when I asked my sister-in-law, who was researching our family's genealogy, if she had come across anything about my great aunt. She said, "You know she's on the internet." No, I didn't know. It wouldn't have occurred to me that my ancient aunt, who might be an afterthought in family stories, was on the internet.

Sure enough, though, there she was on Wikipedia, complete with picture and multi-sourced biography. I also found information about the Powys Society, which holds annual meetings alternately in Dorset, England, and Llangollen, Wales, to discuss the writings of Alyse's husband, Llewelyn Powys, and his brothers, John Cowper and T. F. Powys, as well as the writings and influence of Alyse Gregory and other Powys' luminaries. I discovered that the Sundial Press in Sherborne, England, had just republished two of Aunt Alyse's novels, *Hester Craddock* and *King Log and Lady Lea.*

My journey began. I bought the novels and booked my travel to the Powys Society's annual conference. A wondrous world, so nourishing to my soul, opened up. Delightful friends from around the world discussed my favorite literature with me. Each summer, I now explore exquisite sites in the British Isles en route to and from the conference. In August 2019, I opened the Powys Society Annual Conference, with a presentation titled, "Alyse Gregory: Out of the Shadows."

If you feel even a slight inclination to find out about a relative's or historical figure's life, follow that urge. A higher power guides you. Pursue the twists and turns of the journey, for in all likelihood, it will not be a linear trip from point A to point B. The byways will provide unexpected pleasures and reveal truths that make you draw in your breath.

Your intuition and trust are of paramount importance. To key into your destination, you will need to listen to the small, yet urgent voice within you for direction. Then, you must trust your instincts—which is not always an easy thing to do.

The journey will be a reward in and of itself because you are following your passions, your inner voice, and the voices of those who have gone before you. It may also lead to truths that will heal your lineage and stories that the world needs to hear.

Author Christine Halvorson leads workshops on how to unearth and write intriguing stories about your family's hidden past. According to Halvorson, amateur genealogists too often conduct valuable research only to let it lie fallow in file boxes and attics. Halvorson wrote her book, *Inmate*, based on her family's secret that when her great-grandfather died in the 1918 Spanish flu epidemic, her family committed her grandmother to a home for delinquent girls. *Inmate* depicts her grandmother's gripping backstory.

Find out more about Halvorson's books and workshops at her Facebook page, "Author Christine Halvorson," or ask to join her closed Facebook group called "Spinning Gold: Writing Compelling Stories from Family Research."

What if you aren't drawn to any figure from your past or in history? Not to worry—there are many other ways of finding your destiny and power. We will explore these paths together in the following chapters.

DESTINY TALKS JOURNAL PROMPTS

1. Who in your extended family fascinates you? What characteristics and personal gifts do you share?
2. Does a mystery surround a family member? What qualities and/or stories about this family member intrigue you?
3. Where can you find more information about your lineage and the family members who inspire you? If you need help figuring out where to find information, ask a librarian, friends, or a member of a genealogical society. What has your research uncovered?

IV

EXPLORING THE UNKNOWN
METAPHYSICAL NOTES

M etaphysical tools such as astrology, oracle cards, past life regression, and numerology are delightful ways to gain insight into your soul's purpose and to unfetter your voice. My friends have wondered why I, with my profoundly analytical education, seek answers from astrology and the like. I am tempted to give them Hamlet's reply to Horatio, a philosophy graduate student, who questions Hamlet about the wisdom of believing in a message from an insubstantial ghost:

> "There are more things in Heaven and Earth,
> Horatio, than are dreamt of in your philoso-
> phy." (*Hamlet*, 1.5.167–8)

Actually, it doesn't matter to me whether or not we can prove the truth of astrology or communication from another world. The unknown is just that: unknowable.

Instead, I ask two questions of metaphysical information:

1. <u>Does it make sense?</u> The information has to be reasonable in terms of understanding my life and future. It may challenge my beliefs, perhaps even strain credulity, but it shouldn't be beyond the pale. If the information seems outlandish, I will tuck it away and examine its wisdom over the coming days. I will not accept it as the gods' given truth. After all, another human with all his or her biases concocted the philosophy.

2. <u>Is it useful information that will help me evolve positively?</u> I need to perceive that the guidance springs from a loving source. I believe that the truth comes to us with kindness. Its purpose is to lift us up, not to drag us down. Many times, I've faced a metaphysical reading thinking that I will learn how wrong-headed I've been, and that poverty and heartache are right around the corner. Never, in the hundreds of readings I've done using various modalities, has this been the case. It should never be the case for you, as well. If it is, jettison the information and seek a new reader.

Meta means beyond or transcending. Metaphysics refers to the study of phenomena that cannot be observed, events that transcend the physical. It is a branch of philosophy derived from Plato's belief that what exists lies beyond experience.

You can use metaphysical tools to plumb your spirit and hone an invaluable gift: intuition. Intuition, often called the sixth sense, will warn you of dangers and guide you toward your purpose. It will help you know how to make decisions from the perspective of living in accordance with your higher self.

Intuition also lives in the world of the unknown. It's not like the other senses that are easily accessible. Most of us are accustomed to judging reality by seeing, hearing, smelling, touching, or tasting it. Intuition is about "knowing" truth. Our intuition can emanate from our other senses. Some people, for example, are clairvoyant or clairaudient, meaning they see or hear information from other unknowable dimensions. In this way, the other five senses serve intuition.

Those gifted with heightened senses, who may act as mediums to other worlds, believe that you can enhance your intuition with training. There are countless online courses to help you do this. Almost all the world-renowned metaphysicians such as Sandra Anne Taylor, Colette Baron-Reid, James Van Praagh, and John Holland have developed workshops and curricula focused on developing intuitive skills. You can find their courses by Googling their names on the internet.

Metaphysics is a doorway into understanding yourself. It gives you messages from the outside that you can use to understand your inner being. In truth, it reveals information which you already know deep inside. If you see numbers that guide you to be a teacher or a graphic designer, for example, your intuition or your inner guidance system will tell you whether or not this information is worth considering.

I caution you against believing that metaphysical tools such as tarot cards and your solar return astrological chart can tell your future, for two primary reasons. First, you have free will. These tools can give you insights into your current situation and trajectory; however, you have the power to choose to use these insights to either stay your course or change your life's path. The seeds, which can blossom into flowers or rank weeds, are planted today. You can choose which seeds to nourish. Second, if you believe that something is going to happen, you can turn it into a self-fulfilling prophecy. You can make it come true.

Much of modern spiritual teaching is built on the concept that thoughts shape reality. Norman Vincent Peale, Napoleon Hill, Wayne Dyer, Mike Dooley, and countless other motivational authors espouse the power of positive thinking.

Louise Hay built a thought-leading, publishing empire based on her knowledge that our thoughts have the power to heal. She popularized the idea that we can use positive affirmations to create the life of our dreams. Our negative thoughts can also presage our downfall.

The power of thoughts, encompassed in our desires and coupled with intention, can be an unstoppable force. Deepak Chopra posits that it controls our destiny. He quotes from the ancient, mystical text, the *Brihadaranyaka Upanishad*, which states that our desire creates our intention, which creates our will, which creates our deeds, which determines our destiny.

There are hundreds of modalities that might be classified as metaphysics. In the next chapters, I will introduce the practices that have helped me on my journey. If I do not describe a particular modality, it only means that I have not yet explored its depths. It may or may not be useful; I just don't have any experience with it. There are also some tools such as The Passion Test, Byron Katie's The Work, and the Emotional Freedom Technique, which I explore in chapters related to using joy as your GPS and techniques for overcoming limiting beliefs.

DESTINY TALKS JOURNAL PROMPTS

1. Are you drawn to metaphysics? If yes, which subjects pique your curiosity? Which ones have you explored? Which would you like to study?
2. If you are skeptical about metaphysics, why do you doubt its usefulness?

V

PORTAL II TO THE SOUL
METAPHYSICAL TOOLS, PART 1

In the next two chapters, I provide a basic overview of metaphysical disciplines so you can determine if you are interested in learning more about them. If you would like to delve deeper into them, please consult books and internet resources such as those listed in the bibliography and at www.janice-gregory.com.

ASTROLOGY: WHAT'S PLUTO GOT TO DO WITH IT?

Astrology studies the influence of celestial bodies, including the sun, moon, planets, and asteroids, on events and on our lives. This contrasts with astronomy, which explores the physical properties of celestial bodies that scientists can observe.

In astrology, the sun, the moon, and each planet have archetypal qualities:

>Sun—personality, the ego, who you appear
>   to be, your identity
>Moon—emotions, the subconscious, your
>   inner urges, a mother
>Saturn—work, order, lessons, and discipline,
>   a stern father
>Pluto—transformation, the soul's guide
>Mercury—communication, the messenger
>Venus—beauty and love, a goddess
>Mars—action, a warrior
>Jupiter—opportunities for growth and
>   success, a gift giver
>Neptune—inspiration, a dreamer
>Uranus—unexpected events, a liberator or a
>   revolutionist

These celestial bodies traverse the universe and—depending on their relationship to each other and your unique birth date, time, and location—define your characteristics and the events transpiring in your life at a given time.

I know, it's totally hard to believe! Nonetheless, understanding my birth chart and solar returns (the charts that depict the planets' and celestial bodies' alignments on the date of my birth and subsequent birthdays respectively) has given me countless insights into my nature and my life's events. It has also provided me with comfort when everything in my life has gone haywire.

In August 2017, I finally began to write this book. In the back of my mind, I had long wanted to write historical fiction about my great aunt, but as I had never written fiction, I thought I'd tackle a book of nonfiction first. I had loads of experience writing nonfiction and could call on my life experiences for the substance.

As luck, or synchronicity, would have it, deep into writing this book, I received an email from Chandler Bolt's Self-Publishing School promoting a new online course designed to guide students in writing a work of fiction to be completed in ninety days. The course came complete with modular instruction and coaching. I listened to the promotional webinar and was hooked. (You can find out more about Self-Publishing School's courses and appropriate links at www.janicegreg-ory.com.)

What was happening? For years, I'd skirted committing to writing because I needed to make money, lacked confidence in my skills, thought I needed to do something more practical, and a hundred other excuses. Now, though I still had those excuses, I was suddenly writing two books—one nonfiction, and the other historical fiction.

I consulted my astrologer, Allice, who said I was right on track. For the next year or so, Pluto, the planet of transformation, was forecast to dance back and forth with Mercury, the planet of communication. The upshot was that my relationship with communicating was destined to be transformed.

I have no idea if this means that I will no longer deny the voice inside me that has always wanted to be an author, if I'll be successful or not, or indeed, if Pluto is going to transform my communication skills. We humans are left to interpret the movements of the celestial bodies and to make use of the information to shape our destiny. In this case, I chose to follow my writing muses. I can adjust my course as events warrant. It comforts me to think that maybe I am supposed to be writing, and maybe I'll succeed in producing something of note.

In 2019, when I consulted Allice about my solar return and told her I was writing this book on destiny, she responded, "Yay!"

"Yay?" I said.

"Yes, this year your sun is conjunct to Mercury, the planet of knowledge and communication (meaning that they appear in the sky at roughly the same time in the same place). They are in the third house, which is the house of knowledge and communication, and which Mercury rules. You're right on track."

I interpret Allice's remark to mean that in 2019 the sun, the outward expression of who I am, had a positive working relationship with Mercury, the planet of communication.

Houses in astrology represent different areas of your life, for example, finances, career, family, etc. When a planet is located in a particular house, it impacts that aspect of your life. In this case, the sun and Mercury influenced my experiences related to knowledge and communication.

Planets don't predict exactly what will happen, but from my experience, they align with what transpires to give us a deeper appreciation of our journey.

For the present, I have ceased writing historical fiction. Rather, I plan to delve deeper into creating personal legacies and lineage healing in my next nonfiction book. Who knows, though? With Mercury dancing back and forth in my chart, I may eventually decide on another course.

Your Chart: Lots of Interacting Forces

I've always said "no" to becoming an astrologer because it seems so complex. There are ten celestial bodies, twelve astrological signs, and twelve houses. Each planet represents a life force that takes on different characteristics depending upon the house it lives in and the sign which influences that house. How the planets are aligned with each other (e.g., trined, sextiled, squared, in karmic knots, etc.) and how they traverse the sky will impact your life differently.

Whoa, way too complex to learn. However, they say that when the student is ready, the teacher will appear. Somehow, Debra Silverman recently turned up in my email inbox. She has a very clear way of explaining key concepts related to your life's destiny. Let's take just four: the sun sign, the rising sign, the sign at your midheaven, and the moon's sign, all at the time of your birth. We will also consider the elements where these signs reside: earth, water, fire, and air.

You can obtain a free chart to ascertain where these signs are in your natal astrological chart by going to www.astro.com, or you can Google free astrological birth charts and check out other sites. You will need to know the location, date, and time, as near as possible, of your birth. These details are stated on the long form of your birth certificate, which you can usually obtain from the administrative offices of the town, city, or state where you were born.

Many popular horoscope interpretations only describe the influence of your sun, which represents your ego (how you outwardly appear to others). It is located in one of the twelve houses—that is, in one of the slices of the "pie" in your chart. The ascendant, your rising sign, noted by the letters "asc" in the chart, is on the outside perimeter of your chart, where the number nine is located on a clock. It represents your soul or spirit, which infuses your chart and will infuse your life. It may or may not be in the same sign and element as your sun. Therein lies a tale.

As noted, each of the zodiac signs is associated with an element: fire, earth, air, and water. They share the characteristics symbolized by these elements. Fire signs—Aries, Leo, and Sagittarius—are energetic, bright, and engaging, like a fire's flames. Earth signs—Taurus, Virgo, and Capricorn—are practical, dependable, and appropriately down-to-earth. If a planet resides in an air sign—Aquarius, Gemini, and Libra—its energy is characterized by thinking and communicating. Finally, the water signs—Pisces, Cancer, and Scorpio—are emotional, deep, and caring.

Here is a basic list of the signs in the zodiac, their symbolic representation, elements, and positive and negative characteristics. You can use this information to interpret the harmonious and countervailing forces in your chart. See if your sun and ascendant signs might work together or not.

Zodiac Sign	Symbol	Element	Personality Traits
Aries	The Ram ♈	Fire	Action-oriented, leads and inspires, not given to introspection
Taurus	The Bull ♉	Earth	Dependable, solidly grounded, sensual, can be stubborn and resistant to change

Zodiac Sign	Symbol	Element	Personality Traits
Gemini	The Twins ♊	Air	Fast-moving, fast-thinking, talkative, can have contradictory characteristics that represent both the good and the bad of a trait, such as being flexible vs. unreliable
Cancer	The Crab ♋	Water	Empathetic, lovable, adaptable, easily distracted, can be overly sensitive and dependent
Leo	The Lion ♌	Fire	Dramatic, self-confident, charismatic, a leader, loyal, can be narcissistic and stubborn
Virgo	The Virgin ♍	Earth	Into beauty and perfection, detail-oriented, analytic, practical, organized, can be inflexible and critical

Zodiac Sign	Symbol	Element	Personality Traits
Libra	The Scales ♎	Air	Balanced, social, idealistic, friendly, attractive, can be indecisive and self-sacrificing
Scorpio	The Scorpion ♏	Water	Mysterious, intense, persevering, powerful, sexual, charismatic, can be deceptive and cruel
Sagittarius	The Archer ♐	Fire	Seekers of meaning, independent, adventurous, enthusiastic, fun, honest, can be dogmatic and not given to commitment
Capricorn	The Goat ♑	Earth	Slow and steady achievers, practical, reserved, responsible, ambitious, self-disciplined, concerned about helping others and the greater good, can be cold, rigid, and judgmental

Zodiac Sign	Symbol	Element	Personality Traits
Aquarius	The Water-Bearer ♒	Air	Innovators, eccentric, future-oriented, non-conformists, intellectually independent, care about humanity more than individuals, can be aloof and touchy
Pisces	The Fish ♓	Water	Intuitive, sensitive, spiritual, deep, idealistic, kind, can be impractical and introverted

The zodiac sign on the top perimeter of your chart, twelve on a clock, was directly overhead when you were born. It is indicated by the letters "mid" for midheaven. It represents the energy influencing your career choice especially later in life. For example, if your midheaven is in a fire sign, your life assignment is to show up and be bold. This could be in almost any field, though one naturally thinks of activists, actors, and leaders. Healers, therapists, and caretakers have their midheaven in water signs, while the midheavens of communicators, such as writers and speakers, are in air signs. Those who bring stability and grounding to others' lives, such as financial managers and organizers, have midheavens in earth signs.

Then there is your moon's sign. Your moon is your unconscious. According to Silverman, it's more powerful than the sun because the unconscious often directs your conscious actions without you knowing it. Its heart overrules reason. She gives the example of your sun saying that you're going on a diet today and your moon saying, "Oh no, you're not. You're going to eat this piece of chocolate."

Once you know the basic characteristics of the signs, planets, and elements, you can speak the language of archetypes, a kind of shorthand for understanding others' driving energies.

I have a friend, Nicole, who said that one of her greatest insights in marriage counseling came when she learned that her sun in Virgo, an earth sign, and her moon in Sagittarius, a fire sign, are almost the exact opposite of her husband's ruling energies. His sun is in Aries, a fire sign, and his moon is in Virgo, an earth sign. When her husband is cautious about change or adventures, because his moon is in Virgo, Nicole is patient, knowing the exact words to say, because she recognizes Virgo's influence, as it rules her sun.

Does this pique your interest? There are hundreds of books explaining astrology, the meaning of the signs, elements, houses, and planets. This is the most basic example from Silverman's work. To learn more about Silverman's teachings, go to her website, www.debrasilvermanastrology.com, where she offers astrology courses for all levels of learners.

The Complete Idiot's Guide to Astrology also provides an excellent introduction to the subject. Do not be fooled by its title. I have often found that the *Idiot Guides* offer clear introductions to various subjects.

Here's a fun way to remember the basic characteristics of the zodiac signs. On her Instagram page, the astrologer, Tosha

Silver, imagined the following tongue-in-cheek, but completely apt, descriptions of the human expressions of the sun signs:

> Aries: I'm tougher than u
> Taurus: I want more than u
> Gemini: I'm smarter than u
> Cancer: I feel more than u
> Leo: I'm more fun than u
> Virgo: I'm neater than u
> Libra: I'm nicer than u
> Scorpio: I'm hotter than u
> Sagittarius: I'm faster than u
> Capricorn: I'm more driven than u
> Aquarius: I'm (way) weirder than u
> Pisces: I'm more psychic than u

My sun and ascendant (rising sign) are in Aquarius, my moon is in Cancer, and Sagittarius is at my midheaven. In other words, my ego and spirit are unique, my subconscious cares deeply, and my career is enhanced by a blazing, adventurous spirit.

NUMEROLOGY: YOUR DESTINY IS IN YOUR NUMBERS

Almost as mystifying as the accuracy of astrology is how numbers can illuminate your life path, your soul's calling, the characteristics of periods of your life, and your destiny. Numerologists will tell you that the accuracy of the numbers is based on Pythagoras's work. Pythagoras, as you may recall from geometry, is the Greek philosopher who gave us the Pythagorean theorem, which states that the square of the length of the hypotenuse of a right triangle equals the sum of the squares of the lengths of the other two sides. Followers of Pythagoras believe, among other things, in the mystical power of numbers.

Do numbers have mystical powers? Maybe, maybe not. All I know is that the proof is in the pudding. When I first calculated my numbers, I was amazed at how accurately they described my personal traits and life trajectory.

Each number from one to nine has a specific energy. All numbers greater than nine can be reduced by adding the digits within the numbers (so that 10 becomes 1 + 0, which is 1). Repeating numbers such as 11, 22, etc. are considered master numbers with heightened energy derived from the individual digits.

Some double-digit numbers such as 13, 14, 16, and 19 are considered Karmic Debt Numbers. The number one refers to self-centered abuse in a former life of the energy contained in the number following the one. So, for example, if you have the number 19 in your chart, it indicates that you misused spirituality for your own gain in a prior life.

Numbers are also assigned to letters in the alphabet so that A is one, B is two, until you reach I, which is nine. Then you begin assigning the numbers over again so that J is one, K is two and so on. In this way, you can assign numbers to a name and reduce it to a single digit. Michael, for example, is 4+9+3+8+1+5+ 3, which equals the master number 33, which can be further reduced to 6.

Here are the number equivalents for letters in the alphabet:

A,J,S=1	B,K,T=2	C,L,U=3	D,M,V=4
E,N,W=5	F,O,X=6	G,P,Y=7	H,Q,Z=8
I,R=9			

Some of the basic energies assigned to the numbers seem intuitively obvious. One is a number of leaders, someone who acts primarily on his or her own. Two is a number of partnerships, someone who relates well to others and so forth. Wherever a number appears in your chart, it carries the same energy and meaning. The energy has both positive and negative characteristics depending upon how it manifests in a person's life. Here are the basic positive and negative energies of the numbers:

1—leader, spirited, initiating, self-centered
2—partner, sensitive, supportive, passive, self-sacrificing
3—joyous, exuberant, optimistic, lucky, scattered, unpredictable
4—hardworking, disciplined, systematic manager, rigid
5—impulsive, adventurous, energetic, unfocused, chaotic
6—loving, responsible, a time of marriage or divorce, martyr
7—mystical, scientific, introvert, solitary, aloof
8—powerful, achiever, money-making, successful, materialistic
9—transforming, completing, serving mankind, challenging

Numerology helps you gain an understanding of your life by examining the numbers in your birth name and birth date. There are numerous calculations that can be derived from these numbers.

The sum of the numbers in your birth name—your name exactly as it is spelled on your birth certificate—reveals your destiny. The sum of the numbers in your birth date reveals your life path. The sum of the number of the vowels in your name indicates your soul's purpose or heart's desire.

If you add your destiny and life path numbers together you will get your life realization number, which describes the energy that rules the latter half of your life. Also, each year, month, and day since your birth carries a particular energy for you.

Michelle Obama, for example, was named Michelle LaVaughn Robinson when she was born on January 17, 1964. Both her destiny and life path number, 11/2, are the master number of an inspirer who can transform the lives of others. Moreover, her life realization number is the master builder number 22/4. This is a rare number combination and augurs the life of someone who will be famous and have a significant, uplifting impact on the world stage. Obama's lower vibration numbers, that is, the 2, derived from her master number 11, and the 4, derived from her master number 22, reveal a person who is sensitive and hardworking. Her soul's purpose is the number 8, the number of a successful high achiever.

It takes a skilled numerologist to paint a complete picture of your destiny, your life path, and essence because there are so many calculations that describe your soul and the energies that will influence your time on this earth. However, in my experience, the resulting insights from this picture are well worth investing in a reading. Like astrology, numerology often confirms what you already know, giving you insights into how to manage your life forces.

When I first began readings, I had a client where the number five figured prominently in her chart. The shadow side of five is that it can be a number of addiction and sexual promiscuity. Some numerologists refer to five as the number of the one-night stand. I hesitated to ask my client, who seemed quite proper and in control of her life, whether either of these applied to her. Nevertheless, I did ask. Much to my surprise, she had experienced both periods of addiction and hooking up with serial sexual partners for one-night stands.

Given the information that her behavior was revealed in her numbers, she could decide how to manage it. I suppose it's a bit like finding that you have a gene which gives you the propensity for addiction. Forewarned is forearmed.

DESTINY TALKS JOURNAL PROMPTS

<u>Astrology</u>

As previously pointed out, you can obtain a free birth chart, which shows where the astrological signs were at the date, time, and location of your birth by going to www.astro.com, or you can Google free astrological charts and check out other sites.

1. Fill in the blank with the appropriate sign from your birth chart:
   Your sun sign_____
   Your ascendant (rising) sign_____
   Your moon sign_____
   The sign at your midheaven_____

2. What characteristics of your sun and ascendant signs describe you? Do their energies reinforce each other or clash?

3. What is the energy from the sign at your midheaven that is affecting your career path?

Numerology

1. What is your destiny number? _____

This is the reduced sum of the numbers in your birth name as written on your birth certificate. Use the chart in this chapter to change the letters in your name to numbers. Add the numbers, and then continue reducing them until you have a single digit.

Here is an example of how to do this. Oprah Winfrey's birth name is Orpah Gail Winfrey. It's Orpah, not Oprah, on her birth certificate. She was named after a character in the Bible's Book of Ruth.

If you substitute numbers for letters, her name translates to 6+9+7+1+8=31 for Orpah, 7+1+9+3=20 for Gail, and 5+9+5+6+9+5+7=46 for Winfrey.

Oprah's three names reduce to the numbers 31, 20, and 46, which can be added together and reduced as (3+1) +(2+0) +(4+6) =16, and then finally reduced by adding 1+6=7. Oprah's destiny number is 7, the number of a spiritual leader.

2. What is your life path number? _____

This is the reduced sum of the numbers in your birth date. For example, you can write December 1, 1976 as 12/01/1976. You can then add the numbers in this date as follows, (1+2) +(0+1) +(1+9+7+6) =27 You can reduce 27 further by adding 2+7=9. Nine, which is the number of a humanitarian, is the reduced life path number for December 1, 1976.

3. Free write or journal on what your astrological signs and numbers say about your personality, life path, and destiny.

VI

PORTAL II TO THE SOUL
METAPHYSICAL TOOLS, PART 2

PSYCHICS AND MEDIUMS: THURSDAYS
WITH KATIE

I won a session with Katie Benway at a silent auction benefiting the Music School in Manchester, New Hampshire. Her company's name is Intrepid Eleven. Since I'm a numerologist, I knew that eleven was the master number of spiritual guidance. Intrepid, of course, means fearless. *How cool,* I thought. *A fearless guide.*

I have always been fascinated with psychics. Like many, I've wanted to peer into my future. Would the man of my dreams find me? What is my perfect career? Four years and several remarkable sessions later, I still don't know the answer to these questions—but I am living a richer, more meaningful, and joyous life filled with wonder and anticipation. I've also been saved from self-sabotaging behavior.

I struck gold when I met Katie, a lovely brunette in her thirties, professionally dressed, so totally normal looking and wise beyond her years. She exudes warmth and asks penetrating questions that take you places you didn't know you wanted to go.

"Did your mother lose a child when she was very young?"

I searched my memory. "She had an abortion in the 1950s because, in her first trimester, she had German measles, which causes serious birth defects in unborn fetuses."

"I thought so. I'm always careful how I phrase my questions in cases of abortion. I just wanted to let you know that he was a boy and he is with your father now."

So how did she know this? Even if it wasn't true about my brother, Katie had no way of knowing that my father had passed. She gained immediate credibility.

Over the years, we've had delightful conversations with my father, who was a distant, moralistic, authoritarian figure in real life, but is a supportive, relaxed, loving guide now. When my sister resisted visiting my mother, who had advanced dementia, because it was too much for her to bear, my dad urged me from beyond the grave to talk with my sister about "sitting by the well." This was his term for gathering wisdom from being present with my mom.

Of course, I was also anxious to connect with Great Aunt Alyse, whose life I was researching.

"Well," Katie said, "I've never had that happen."

"What do you mean?"

"She's very grumpy. She doesn't want you digging into and exposing her life."

Really?! I was Alyse's fan, and she had chosen me. I wanted the world to know what a gifted writer and remarkable person she was. She'd sacrificed her talents to follow her husband, Llewelyn Powys, an incorrigible libertine, whose literary reputation she'd helped build.

In subsequent readings, Alyse's attitude toward me softened. She has encouraged me to learn about my story through understanding hers. Hers is a classic tale of a courageous, independent thinker striving to realize herself in the first wave of feminism in the 1920s. Ultimately, she was undone by her lack of self-confidence, her hypersensitivity, and her self-criticism.

Mine is the story of coming of age in the sixties (the second wave of feminism), trying to find myself without goal posts, and maturing in the anti-feminist, misogynist period that followed women gaining success in the professions. I, too, suffer from a lack of self-confidence. I constantly second-guess my decisions and, like Alyse, am often excessively judgmental and self-critical.

But the end of my story has not been written. As the #metoo movement reveals society's misogyny and younger women claim their power, I am gaining insights through Alyse's story and writing my final chapters.

Like the magical bag of wind blowing into the sails of Odysseus's ship, my journey has been greatly aided by Katie's connections to the afterworld. She has given the unknowable—the reflections of my ancestors—a voice which has lodged inside me.

Katie is not the first psychic or medium from whom I have sought wisdom. I have had sessions with both little known and famous psychics who have provided me with various insights.

Katie, though, converses in real time with my dead relatives and spirit guides so that I can probe their insights into my present life. She has written *Ignite Your Intrepid Soul: A Courageous Home for Your Heart* to guide our spiritual journey. At her website, www.intrepideleven.com, you can book an individual session or join Fireside with the Soul, a transformative six-month program for creating a deep, healing, and inspirational connection with your soul.

If you are inclined to seek self-knowledge through a psychic and/or medium, keep looking until you find the professional whose work resonates with your preferences. Katie's style does not match everyone's needs. You need to find your own translator of the afterworld, one who is in sync with where you are and where you want to go.

No sooner had I finished writing this than I spoke with my friend Leslie, who had an extraordinary session with Colleen Frances, a psychic/medium energy healer. Colleen markets herself primarily as a grief healer, but her gifts defy this description.

Colleen's soul talks to yours. She confronts dark energies in order to banish them. In Leslie's session, she saw a huge muzzle that penetrated into Leslie's neck and which was secured by a leather halter surrounding her shoulders and back. It had been placed there by her sister.

No wonder Leslie couldn't complete the book she'd been writing for the past five years. She is a talented writer and original thinker and had all the content written, but couldn't organize the material to finish it. Family dynamics were holding her back. Leslie and I were amazed by Colleen's insights.

Since the reading with Colleen and a subsequent astrological reading with Allice Haidden, Leslie's writing has taken off. She's following an organized outline and is on track to publish her book within a year's time. Her persona, meanwhile, is noticeably calmer.

PAST LIFE REGRESSION

Exploring your past lives through past life therapy or regression analysis can also provide healing insights into your present circumstances and, thus, a way to consciously influence your destiny. The healer, in this case, hypnotizes the client by putting her into a deeply relaxed state. Through guided meditation, the healer leads the client back into her past lives to uncover experiences that profoundly impact her present life.

Dr. Brian Weiss popularized this healing modality with his 1988 publication of *Many Lives, Many Masters: The True Story of a Prominent Psychiatrist, His Young Patient, and the Past-Life Therapy that Changed Both Their Lives.* Since this time, he has helped tens of thousands of people through his workshops, individual sessions, CDs, and subsequent publications. His is a gentle, spiritual approach which inspires faith in his guidance.

Weiss did his undergraduate studies at Columbia University, received his medical degree in psychiatry from Yale University, and became head of psychiatry at Mount Sinai Medical Center in Miami, Florida. His epiphany occurred while he was treating Catherine, his psychiatric patient, with hypnotherapy.

Catherine suffered from debilitating anxieties and recurring nightmares. Weiss thought that he would find the root cause of her phobias in early childhood experiences. Instead, under hypnosis, Catherine relayed traumatic experiences from as far back as 1863 B.C. Soon after reliving these experiences under hypnosis, Catherine's problems in her present life began to disappear. Her lives seemed to be linked. Catherine, who was afraid of water in her present life, remembered drowning in a tidal wave in a past life. The hypnotic experience, now termed "past life regression," cured Catherine of her fear of water.

Initially, Weiss could not believe what he was hearing and seeing in Catherine's treatment. His scientific training and analytical mind sent him searching for alternative medical explanations. He resisted believing in even the existence of past lives, not to mention their healing powers and messages that Catherine said came through master spirits.

He was convinced, however, when Catherine gave him information about his dead father and infant son that she couldn't have possibly known. The rest, as they say, is history. Weiss's book has become a classic and has sold more than a million copies. He is internationally renowned for his teachings. He has brought past life therapy from the fringes of therapeutic work into the mainstream. Most importantly, he has brought healing to untold numbers of sufferers.

If Weiss had chosen another destiny, the world would be different. If he had chosen to discount Catherine's experiences—which would have been reasonable, given his background and training—his teachings might never have reached a mass audience. Perhaps another therapist could have made similar discoveries and popularized them. We will never know.

THE AKASHIC RECORDS

The Akashic Records also provide a portal for accessing the past in order to influence the future. According to Sandra Anne Taylor, a modern-day psychic and medium, Akasha is the Sanskrit word meaning ether, space, and sky. It was first popularized by H.P. Blavatsky, who co-founded the Theosophical Society in the late 19th century. Blavatsky used it to refer to Divine Consciousness, the source of all energy and life. Alfred Percy Sinnett added the word "records" to Akasha. He employed the term in his 1884 book, *Esoteric Buddhism*, to explain the Buddhist belief in the permanency of the Akashic archives.

As Taylor explains, the Akashic Records are fields of energy that contain all the technical, creative, and scientific knowledge from the past, present, and future. Everything that has happened or will happen is contained in this energetic field.

Through the use of meditation, Akashic tarot cards, or other methodologies, you can gain access to the Akasha. Then, using creative visualization and your thoughts, which are sources of energy, you can change your future in the records and in real life.

Taylor explains how you can go into a meditative state, invoke the spiritual wisdom of the records, and gain intuitive knowledge about your life. If you picture a large screen in front of you, you can then project the image of what you'd like to happen in your life. For example, if you would like to buy a house, you would imagine the house with specific details, such as color, style, size, amenities, and location in the middle of the screen. You might then picture yourself walking up to the house with a set of keys that belongs to you.

You need to feel the joy, gratitude, and any other emotions you'd experience upon owning the house. The more intensely you let the scene evoke these emotions, the higher the energetic vibrations you will create, and the more likely the events will become part of the Akashic Records and your future reality. Be sure to place yourself in the picture so that it becomes part of your records.

QUANTUM MYSTICISM

Quantum physics is the study of matter at the subatomic level. In quantum physics, particles can be seen in two places at the same time and are viewed as both discrete entities and as a wave, simultaneously. In quantum physics, there is no distinct boundary between objects. The observer determines how particles and objects are seen.

Quantum mysticism relates quantum physics to spirituality and consciousness. It can explain how you can alter your Akashic Records. Since your consciousness creates reality, you can choose what you believe, and reality will shift accordingly. Taylor's book, *Quantum Success: The Astounding Science of Wealth and Happiness*, explains this phenomenon.

DESTINY TALKS JOURNAL PROMPTS

1. Have you ever gone to a reader or psychic/medium? What were the circumstances? What did you learn about yourself?

2. Are you inclined to seek out a reader or psychic/medium's insights? If yes, what has kept you from doing so? Are there particular types of readings you are interested in? Why or why not?

VII

PORTAL III TO YOUR SOUL
YOUR LIFE EXPERIENCES

TRADITIONAL APPROACHES

Y ou don't need astrologists, numerologists, or tarot card readers to understand your destiny. An equally valid way is to dig into understanding your life on your own, or with the help of friends, family, and/or a counselor.

A fun way to start is to draw a timeline or picture of your life. Enter significant events, such as moves, relationships, schools, jobs, marriages, divorces, births, deaths, etc. You can make the picture as elaborate as you choose. You want enough detail so you can analyze what happened, but not so much that the details overwhelm you and obscure the larger picture. There is no right way to do this. Just do what feels best.

If you are more inclined toward writing, music, or dance, you can journal, write a song, or choreograph a dance about your experiences. At this point, you are accessing the right part of your brain, the part that is creative and imaginative. Add feelings to your creative piece, noting joy, anger, excitement, fear, or whatever emotions the event evokes.

This can be an elaborate undertaking. After all, people write 350-page memoirs, compose CDs, fill art galleries, and compile multiple photograph albums of their lives. Understanding your destiny is a lifelong, iterative journey. Many of us wait until we are retired to let our creative impulses run free—to access the wellspring of our being. How much more liberating and instructive it would be to do this earlier in our life's journey.

Your creative take on your life will provide insights into its trajectory and where your destiny is headed if you continue along the same path. It will show you what brings you great joy and what fills you with sadness, rage, or grief. Your task is to see the patterns, to understand your choices, and to ask questions. Then you can assess what to augment and what to eschew as you move forward.

You should look at the paths not taken, as well as those you chose to follow. Are there interests you abandoned in early childhood, for whatever reason? Two interests that I've carried around for fifty years (oh my goodness, I'm old!) were curiosity about my great aunt and the desire to be a writer. These weren't huge, overwhelming desires where I knew that I wanted to be a writer and would write every chance I could get. No, they were seedlings that I never nurtured. When I grew older, the seedlings pushed through the concrete pavement that had kept them encased. I became obsessed with my great aunt's legacy. I chased it down in England and at the Beinecke Library at Yale University. And now I'm writing about it here—and will again, in future books.

Influential People in Your Life

The most influential people in your life often change over time. These people reflect who you are, your values, and attitudes. Consider the five people you interact with most. What do you value about them? How do you wish they would change? Are your interactions mostly positive, or do they stress you out?

Now look back at who you mostly interacted with in your childhood, or just five to ten years ago. You can pick whatever time frame reveals significant changes. It may be that the cadre of folks who you have significant relationships with has remained relatively stable over time, or perhaps your friend group has changed dramatically in recent years. The questions to ask are: Who has stayed by your side, and why? What do these people say about who you were, then and now?

Think about your life going forward. Are there relationships or aspects of relationships that you'd like to change? Are you open to new friends? Where might you find them? Understanding the principal people in your life will tell you about your core values and interactive patterns. Once you understand the roles that different people play in your life, you can consciously decide whether or not you want to change, encourage, discourage, or add certain relationships. It may not always be easy for you to accomplish the changes you envision, but at least you will know how you'd like to proceed. This is the first step toward embracing the relationships of your future.

Soul Conversations

Another way to use the present to mine the past and to create a more ideal future is through soul conversations. These deep discussions with friends, family, coaches, and counselors may guide you to rewrite your narrative. You'll see your past differently, which will, in turn, create a new future.

Soul conversations can occur spontaneously as you catch up with a friend over a cup of coffee or through a counseling session which delves into life issues. In order for our souls to truly connect, however, we need to be able to interact in real time. This precludes texting or email. You need to see the other person's expressions so that you can fully gauge her reactions to your conversation.

Poets describing courtly love in the 16th century portrayed the eyes as the gateway to the soul. This explains why lovers can gaze endlessly into each other's eyes. It's hard to hide how you truly feel from someone whose piercing gaze is set on seeing you.

In a soul conversation, each individual is committed to hearing what the other is saying and to reacting with authenticity and compassion, bringing in his own experiences only when they can shed light on an issue. We need to honor each other's souls.

These discussions do not have to be all darkness and intensity. How much fun is it to share laughter in recognition of shared human foibles?! In fact, the greater the range of emotions the conversation evokes, the more memorable and compelling the discussion will be.

Some questions you might explore are:

1) What were you like as a child, teenager, or young adult?
2) How does the other person view a significant event or relationship, past or present, in your life?

3) What brings you great joy? What's coming up that you're excited about doing? Why?

4) If you've completed a creative depiction of your life, how does another interpret it?

You undoubtedly have your answers to these questions, but do your perceptions jive with those who knew you at the time? You might find some surprising insights.

Recently the validity of eyewitness testimony has come under question because multiple witnesses at an accident scene can demonstrably see quite different events. Each witness brings his own perspective, his own filter, to what he sees. Similarly, we have interpreted our life events to fit a picture that we have of ourselves. Who is to say that this is the correct interpretation or right picture? We can choose a different picture with different implications, if we like.

The questions that ask what we're excited about doing can point us in the direction of greater happiness. We merely need to recognize joy-filled activities and relationships and consciously incorporate more of them into our lives.

A singularly rewarding aspect of being a coach or counselor is sharing soul conversations with your client. In the best sessions, you are both intensely vested in understanding the client's life issues and resolving them. Together, you bring forth the very best human qualities: compassion and creative brainstorming, with which you can improve the human condition. If you make your client's life better, you are making the client's social network—and perhaps your own life—better as well.

A whole new field of epigenetics has shown that the shape of a gene is not immutable. It will change depending on its environment. In the movie, *What the Bleep Do We Know!?*, an intriguing experiment illustrates this supposition. Masaru Emoto, a Japanese scientist, demonstrates how experimenters can transform the very molecules of water by consistently directing negative or positive messages to the water. The implication is that if you behave positively toward your friends and family, they will change positively. The changes can ripple out into society.

MEDITATION

At the other end of the spectrum from sharing soul conversations with others is going deep within yourself to find your truth through meditation. The newsletter, *Healthline.com*, describes twelve generally agreed-upon benefits of meditation. Meditation:

1. Reduces stress
2. Controls anxiety
3. Promotes emotional health
4. Enhances self-awareness
5. Lengthens attention span
6. May reduce age-related memory loss
7. Can generate kindness
8. May help fight addictions
9. Improves sleep
10. Helps control pain
11. Can decrease blood pressure
12. Is easy and inexpensive to do

Many websites and gurus, including Deepak Chopra and a host of Hay House authors, can instruct you in meditation.

Hay House is the leading publisher of spiritual self-help books. The relevant websites, where you can search for instruction and meditations, are www.deepakchopra.com and www.hayhouse.com.

Meditation can incorporate several different processes, from sitting still with your eyes closed to guided meditations, where a teacher helps you visualize an experience. When a guide first suggested introducing meditation into my demanding schedule, he wisely recommended that I begin with a meditation practice that included movement.

"I can see that your mind is much too busy to meditate quietly without struggle," he said. "Why don't you begin by taking up yoga, or a walking meditative practice?"

I've gone back to this suggestion time and again as my life circumstances and goals have changed. For ten years, I would free write a journal entry in the morning for thirty minutes in the fashion that Julia Cameron recommends in *The Artist's Way*. Then, because so many of the spiritual authors I followed swore by meditation's transformative powers, I thought that if I really wanted to know who I was, I should meditate. I didn't have time for both writing and meditating before I began my day, so I put aside my morning writing practice.

For the next five years, I meditated every day for twenty minutes. I would settle into my overstuffed leather chair each morning, turn off my phone, and zone out. Sometimes the time would drag, but as my practice matured, I often found the time would pass in a nanosecond.

When I decided I wanted to write a book, I returned to journaling. I thought I could free write four mornings a week and meditate the other three days. It hasn't quite transpired that way.

At first, it felt strange not to meditate. I didn't exactly miss it, but my life definitely changed. Before long, I began walking around my condo. Ostensibly, this was to meet the requirements of my Fitbit: 10,000 steps each day. What I soon realized, however, was that I was walking and meditating, sometimes not thinking about much of anything, but often noodling through an issue that was preoccupying me, either consciously or subconsciously. My family teases me about walking around in circles, but the monks who practice walking meditations often follow a labyrinth consisting of concentric circles.

I've temporarily given up regular meditating and free writing. Now my morning routines include:

1) Before even rising from bed, consciously reveling in thoughts of things I'm grateful for.
2) Visualizing what I want to accomplish and how I want to feel during the coming day.
3) Drinking a full glass of water—delicious!
4) Walking for twenty minutes or so.
5) Reading an inspirational section of a book or poetry.
6) Perhaps meditating or free writing for ten to twenty minutes depending on how the mood strikes me.
7) Drawing one to three oracle cards to make me think about my life.
8) Having something yummy for breakfast.

I thoroughly enjoy this routine. It starts the day off right. I don't usually do all the steps. It depends on how much time I have before I need to be somewhere.

Since I knew I was going to write about meditating today, I thought I should try once again to sit in stillness for twenty minutes. I wondered if I would start fidgeting and speculating on how much time had passed before even three minutes were over. When I first started meditating, I had to force myself to make it through five minutes. I'm delighted to report that I easily made it through twenty minutes. In fact, I was pissed off at my iPhone's timer for jarring me out of my blissful state.

This all is to say, it doesn't matter what you do. You can choose any routine that fits into your lifestyle, and you can change it up year to year. The goal is to find a practice that inspires you.

DESTINY TALKS JOURNAL PROMPTS

1. As you consider your life, what kinds of experiences would you like to create more of? What kinds of experiences would you like to eliminate from your future? How might you accomplish these changes?

2. Who are the five most influential people in your life today? What do you value about them and your relationship with them? What qualities do they possess that reflect aspects of yourself?

3. What would be your ideal morning routine?

VIII

ISLANDS TO EXPLORE
WORK AND LOVE, PART 1

Sigmund Freud famously summed up life as consisting of work and love. Destiny works its will in these areas. You can find love issues in work and work issues in love, but I'm hard-pressed to think of any more encompassing topics than work and love in which to examine destiny. In this chapter, I'll explore work-related issues. In Chapter IX, I'll look at love.

Work can be broken down broadly into two categories: 1) working for yourself, and 2) working for someone else. Each triggers different personal issues.

WORKING FOR YOURSELF: SMALL
BUSINESS OWNERSHIP

For roughly twenty-five years, I promoted small business development 1) as a means to grow the economy and 2) for the right people, with the right idea, at the right time, as a path to personal fulfillment. The University System of New Hampshire employed me, first as a business professor, then as a business advisor, and finally as the Associate State Director of Program Development for the New Hampshire Small Business Development Center. In this final position, I won several awards for creating innovative training, research, and development programs.

With my biweekly paycheck securely in hand, it was easy for me to coach business owners. I could clearly see their needs and articulate practical steps to grow their businesses.

In 2014, I left the University System to seek another destiny. I eventually opened my own coaching company. It was an arena in which I felt comfortable and had expertise.

"OMG!" as they say. The scales fell from my eyes. The pundits tell you that to be an entrepreneur, you need to be a risk-taker and independent, which may be true. They *don't* tell you that you'll have to face your naked self—all your brilliance, and all your vulnerabilities.

I had moved from New Hampshire to a seacoast town in Massachusetts, which was lovely, but where I knew no one. How to market my wares? Not easy! Hoping to find a quick answer and just the right program, I sought advice from online gurus who had successfully started and scaled their own businesses. They were good at outlining all the right steps. If you just followed their programs, you were bound to succeed beyond your wildest dreams.

I learned a lot about myself. A successful colleague said to me when I was feeling down, "Small business ownership really makes you face your stuff."

Such true words. When you start your own business, it is all about you. It immediately reveals your strengths and weaknesses. If you're coaching others, you need to be sublimely self-confident that you know the answers or how to find them. Self-confidence is not my strong suit. I've never met a decision I couldn't second-guess.

In secondary school and beyond, I often identified with the protagonist in T.S. Eliot's poem, *The Love Song of J. Alfred Prufrock*. Prufrock obsesses over the meaning of his decisions and time:

> Do I dare
> Disturb the universe?
> In a minute there is time
> For decisions and revisions which a minute
> will reverse.

I also loved Hamlet, whose actions were "sicklied o'er with the pale cast of thought." The whole of Shakespeare's three-hour play centers on Hamlet trying to pluck up the courage to avenge his father's death.

Add to this that I was brought up in a New England family, where bragging about your talents and achievements was severely frowned upon.

No wonder I couldn't promote myself. Marketing myself felt like climbing Mount Everest. I knew how to do it, I could research any questions I might have, but the climb seemed fraught with danger, and the summit was so very, very far away.

Is this my destiny? Not to be able to succeed because I can't bring myself to go on Facebook, send out mass emails, or give an elevator speech touting my wares at Chamber of Commerce events? We shall see.

My points are twofold. First, creating your own business will make you squarely face your own issues. Maybe it isn't marketing—maybe it's being organized, knowing how to produce a product you can clearly envision, building supportive relationships, keeping records, managing money, or any number of critical issues. Be forewarned. As Pogo, the comic figure, said, "We have seen the enemy, and it is us!"

Second, in confronting your foibles, you are confronting your destiny. You have choices. You can seek to overcome challenges through various strategies, you can ignore issues, or you can seek alternative work.

Christian Mickelsen, who has successfully built a coaching company empire, states that 92.8 percent of small business success can be attributed to the owner's ability to manage her psychology.

This makes sense. If building your business draws on your internal resources, there are bound to be times when you leap with joy at your success or sink with despair at seeming failures. The obstacles will sometimes be of your own creating, but there can also be ones where fate throws you under the bus. Your business burns down, a business partner cheats you, or your primary customer takes his business elsewhere. Your company is decimated, through no fault of your own.

Your reaction to these challenges determines your destiny. You'll have loads of choices from closing up shop to soldiering on. Each choice will take you down a different path with its own cliffs, mirages, and oases. When you make your decision, you won't be able to peer far down the path to know for certain what the outcome will be. In the next chapter, we'll look at ways to make decisions easier.

Working for Someone Else

Working for a company or organization provides an equally revealing window into your dance with destiny. Here you will bang up against boundaries of another's making. It will be easy to rail against circumstances that seem not to be of your own doing. Who knows, though—maybe your actions in a past life drew these challenges to you, to see what lessons you would learn in this one.

For roughly forty years, I worked for someone else. I rose to be the second-in-command, the one who whispered in Caesar's ear. This was a safe spot for me. I was able to accomplish a lot without having to stand up in front of crowds and say, "We're going to do this." It's true that I didn't get kudos for my great ideas, but neither did I have to risk criticism and failure. I have also received satisfaction for twenty years from helping my colleagues cope with a difficult boss.

Moreover, this gave me space to manage my stressful personal life, including challenging relationships with my then husband and two boundary-defying teenage stepsons.

It was a cop-out. I pretended that I had no responsibility for my boss's and ex-husband's values and choices. I could hide behind the excuse that they were in charge. I never really had to stand up for my choices. I was a victim of circumstance.

If you don't respect a person, supporting them becomes a soul-crushing proposition. I had to leave. Don't think for a moment that either of them cherished the hard work I'd done for them. When the king becomes tired of his counselor, he doesn't reward him with praise; he chops off his head.

The pattern of my relationships in both work and love had such devastating consequences for me that I have spent the past ten years seeking a new destiny. Much to my surprise, 90 percent of my journey has been filled with breathtaking vistas, soul connections, and beckoning experiences. Ten percent of the journey still terrifies me. Can I make it? What devastation lies around the next corner? Will poverty overtake me? Can I really build a successful career and romantic love life before my death bell tolls?

You can be terrifically successful in a job working for someone else. You do not have to mute your voice or leave to succeed. You are exactly where you are meant to be. You need to take stock of what's working and what is causing you stress, your gifts and personal preferences, as well as the work you'd rather someone else do.

In her forthcoming book, *From Burnout to Purpose: Simple Strategies for Soul-fulfilling Approaches to Work,* Gina Calvano gives inspirational and practical advice on creating your "personal brand" and thriving in a corporate setting.

One secret to succeeding is embracing the concept of an *internal* locus of control. This is when you view events through the lens of always being at least partially responsible for what happens to you. If you have an *external* locus of control, you believe that events happen to you randomly, that fate and other people totally control your circumstances.

Research has shown that being a high achiever is correlated with having an internal locus of control. This is logical. If you believe your actions matter, you will generally take steps to achieve your desired future. If you don't believe your actions matter, there's no incentive for you to direct your course.

One night, my father, a successful physician and researcher at Cornell University's medical school, came home from work miffed that his new fur hat had been stolen right off his head as he was walking. He had luxuriated in the hat's protection from the cold, ravaging winter winds coursing down the streets of New York City. Instead of cursing the thief, however, he made two observations. First, that he had taken a route to work that ran through a sketchy, crime-riddled neighborhood. He should have known better than to venture into that neighborhood. Second, he said, he couldn't really blame the thief, who, he opined, must have been cold and lacked the money to buy such a hat. It made sense that the young man would have stolen a fur hat from a man who looked like he could easily afford another one. Here is an example of someone with a strong internal locus of control.

Nevertheless, even if we take the wrong route home, we are not *wholly* responsible for crimes that befall us. Why one person is attacked while another avoids harm in the same circumstance is often inexplicable.

The Hindus explain incomprehensible, unforeseen events as one's karma. An individual cannot avoid experiencing certain events in his present life because his actions in a past life have determined his present fate. It is his karma. There are different forms of karma, including Prarabdha Karma, which dictates that we have certain lessons which we must learn in this lifetime. No matter how much we might like to manifest a different lifestyle, our destiny, in this regard, has already been written. This being said, we, as humans, have no idea which destiny is predetermined and which we can mitigate by our actions.

We can exercise control over how we respond to hurtful events. We can chalk our experiences up to bad luck, blame others, blame ourselves, or look for the hidden lesson. To me, assigning blame, whether to the universe or a person, gets us nowhere. Better to look for the hidden lesson, our Prarabdha Karma. Finding the lesson can be challenging, but it gives us a way to create a positive outcome from a negative event.

Recently, I tripped over a pile of papers on my study floor and fell face-first onto my desk. My jaw and neck were painfully bruised. I was not only hurt but felt frustrated because several events on my schedule demanded attention, and now, I was self-conscious about going out in public with a battered face. I came to terms with my situation by viewing the fall as a warning that I needed to slow down. Instead of scattering my attention by going to various events, I needed to focus on writing an article that I'd been avoiding. After all, I had just tripped over the research for that article.

DESTINY TALKS JOURNAL PROMPTS

1. Assess your work environment. What or who supports you? What stresses you out? How can you change your work environment to make it more supportive? If you can't change the environment, can you change your beliefs about it so that you feel happier?
2. What role do you play in creating your successes and challenges? Is there anything you would change?
3. How can you claim your power and show up authentically? What might be the risks and rewards of doing so?

IX

ISLANDS TO EXPLORE
WORK AND LOVE, PART 2

LOVE

We also face destiny in our primary relationships. Were Romeo and Juliet "star-crossed" lovers whose lives marched inexorably toward their suicides, or did they have some choice in their destiny? It's Shakespeare's genius that he weaves the tale as one of fate. We might not have been drawn into the lovers' drama if it had been cast less cosmically or had unfolded with the protagonists weighing their options and behaving rationally.

I face writing about fate's role in love with trepidation. Relationships seem much more fraught with the unknowable than work. You could argue that it is actually the relationships in work environments that make one's success unpredictable.

I have always marveled that Shakespeare writing in the 17th century, and the Greeks, writing more than 2,000 years ago, could depict human drama that resonates with 21st century audiences. While we now have psychological nomenclature to label human behavior and, indeed, there are certain untenable human behaviors that we can control with drugs, we have made relatively little progress in understanding and mitigating the most destructive human actions.

At the other end of the spectrum, we are inspired by genius and great humanitarian acts that seem almost inhumanly good. Yet we are unable to know for certain how to bring out the good in our fellow man. Why does one person rush to perform a heroic act and another faced with the same circumstances shrink back in fear? We can only speculate.

Our mettle is determined in the arenas of relationships and love. They can provoke the most tender, generous actions, and they can make us into monsters exacting untold destruction.

Here is where self-knowledge, control, and conscious decision-making can determine our destiny. We have choice; free will is ours. We can reflect on a situation or relationship and decide how to act. We can seek revenge or turn the other cheek.

Contemplating the consequences of our choices will illuminate our chosen fate. If we say or tweet hurtful comments about a person, what will we accomplish? Will we truly feel better or feel remorse? Our ego and pride can confuse our answer. The heat of the moment can override our best instincts. But we still have a choice.

These are complex issues. Writers have filled libraries with tomes depicting heroism and villainy. Similarly, psychologists and psychiatrists have spent decades proposing innumerable theories explaining why humans behave the way they do.

I have no set answer except to say that we humans have the capacity to know ourselves and to behave consciously. This is our ballast against raging karma.

We also have the ability to choose what relationships we nurture. It may take until late adulthood before we embrace this notion. We're supposed to love our parents and our siblings. Imagine, however, if you were born into an abusive family. You could spend countless hours and untold suffering trying to right these relationships. In some cases, you might be able to. In others, your best course would be to leave the family you were born into and strike out on your own, perhaps creating a new family out of your friends.

My good friend, Robin, a strong, spiritual, caring soul, was born into a family of "malignant narcissists." She always felt guilty that she wasn't able to please them until a therapist showed her the diagnostic description of a "malignant narcissist." Malignant narcissism is the most extreme form of narcissism which includes self-centered behavior that is antisocial, aggressive, and sadistic. Finally, Robin understood how her siblings' behavior had driven her to the therapist's office and that she was not responsible for, nor could she really influence, their behavior.

Her parents had not protected Robin from her siblings because they didn't know better. They had suffered at the hands of their own large families and couldn't provide the nurturing that Robin's soul craved.

I asked Robin why she thought she'd been born into such a damaged soul group. Her response: "I needed to learn how to value myself and set boundaries."

What then, I wondered, were her siblings gaining from their relationship? What was the purpose of their being part of this family constellation?

The answer isn't clear. What is clear is that Robin's three children are benefiting enormously. Because of Robin's conscious choice to honor herself, she is also honoring her children's souls. Robin's first priority is to let her children know that their feelings matter. She respects the core of their beings. Seeing and honoring another's essence is the very definition of love.

Robin's children, their children, and their children's children will not have to struggle to learn their mother's lessons. They will know their own value and can turn away from people who refuse to acknowledge their innate worthiness.

When you consider that most child abuse victims abuse their own children, you can see how tenacious the behavior that we learn from our families can be. Surely, many of these victims would not consciously choose to perpetuate suffering by punishing their children in the same way they were treated. Yet, to stop this behavioral pattern, they have to recognize that they are the victims of family abuse. Then they have to consciously determine that they will neither abuse their children nor let their children abuse each other. They must muster the self-discipline to change learned, abusive behavior that can easily take over when one is frustrated, angered, or out of control. However, by consciously undertaking this arduous journey, they will give their families the inestimable gift of generational healing in this life and beyond. They will change their families' destinies.

CHOOSE CAREFULLY

Have you ever noticed how you are a different person depending upon whom you are with? Some people may bring out the child in you. With others, you may be serious and philosophical. With some, you may feel your burdens more, while others lighten you up. You will find it easy to share yourself with some people, while in other cases, you'll draw into yourself like the crab that retreats into its shell when touched. You may listen, but you won't share.

Many spiritualists feel that there is no separation between human beings. We are all part of the whole. If this is the case, then others reflect facets of ourselves.

We should select our loved ones and friends carefully, as our selection determines how we feel in our lives—joyful, guilt-ridden, listened to, valued, neglected, ambitious, creative, ignored, funny, or generous, for example. We may have a variety of friends who will bring out the best or worst in us, in different circumstances.

Woe be to us if we don't believe we deserve to feel good. We will pick friends and colleagues who reflect back our feelings of unworthiness. Don't go there! Even if you are filled with self-criticism and doubt, be conscious and pick friends who lift you up.

Also, no matter how you feel, think of your friends' needs as well, and aim to inspire them to be their best. As Kahlil Gibran wrote in *The Prophet:*

> And let your best be for your friend.
> If he must know the ebb of your tide, let him
>   know its flood also.
> For what is your friend that you should seek
>   him with hours to kill?
> Seek him always with hours to live.[1]

---

[1]   Kahlil Gibran, *The Prophet* (New York: Alfred A. Knopf, 1923), 67.

Don't give folks who treat you badly the benefit of the doubt. As Maya Angelou once said, "When people show you who they are, believe them." You may not have much choice in selecting your birth family, but you certainly have choice in picking your friends and your life partner(s). Don't saddle yourself with someone who makes you miserable, even if he or she is rich, famous, attractive, or has some other quality you lust after. Your soul will never be satisfied with such superficial qualities. Don't underestimate your own ability to earn money and fame and to make yourself alluring. You may find the effort you spend in these endeavors is far less stressful than subjugating yourself to another because you desire his or her achievements.

DESTINY TALKS JOURNAL PROMPTS

1. Reflect on your love affairs and friendships. How have you enhanced the quality of experiences with people you love?
2. What could you do more of, or differently, to build stronger relationships? What would be the consequences for your life if you created stronger relationships?

X

GUIDING YOUR JOURNEY: NAVIGATIONAL TOOLS

A HAPPY OR A MISERABLE JOURNEY: THE CHOICE IS MOSTLY YOURS

In his lighthearted song, "Winsome Smile," Chris Smithers tries to cheer up a friend who is mired in heartbreak. He urges his friend to screw his head on right and get out and meet some people. Then Chris admonishes him, "It's hard to believe, but I'm telling you, your mind will soon recover, but you don't want it to. You love this ache and agony 'cause it's noble and it's true. You won't forsake this pain for other lovers. Happiness would fill your mind with misery."

There may be perks to being unhappy. You could be viewed as a noble sufferer. Someone might take pity and help you out. You don't have to worry about anyone bringing you down with jealousy over your good fortune. Nor do you have to have your high spirits dashed by unexpected events. If you're not expecting anything good to happen, you won't be disappointed if it doesn't occur.

Mostly though, if you look for unhappiness, you will find it. And I would argue there aren't many benefits to being miserable. You just have to know someone who suffers from depression to know how debilitating despair can be. J.K. Rowling created one of the most terrifying characters in literature, the dementor, who sucks the life out of humans and wizards alike, based on her experience with depression.

Barring mental illness (discussing clinical depression is beyond the scope of this book), most of us can choose whether or not we want to build a happy life. It may not be easy, especially if we've lived many unhappy years or are suffering from debilitating circumstances, but it can be done.

Shawn Achor, Chief Executive Officer of GoodThink Inc., a consulting firm that advocates fostering positivity and optimism to drive business results, explains that while most of us are born with a happiness set point—that is, a level of equanimity which we will return to once interfering events subside—we can change that set point. It takes a concerted effort, but genes do not determine our temperament, as much as we might suspect. Research indicates that your happiness set point, even if you don't change it, only accounts for 50 percent of your sense of well-being.

Many believe that success breeds happiness. It might, temporarily. The effects, however, are not usually sustained over time. People who attain a coveted goal often feel let down afterward. They wonder, "Is this all there is?"

The overwhelming amount of evidence, amassed by Achor and others, is that the formula is backward. It's not success that leads to happiness; rather, happiness causes success. Be happy first, and you will achieve much more than if you are low-spirited.

We have to decide we truly want what happiness can bring: loving relationships, gratitude, joy, better health, high performance, and career success.

Why would anyone pick unhappiness? As stated above, there are many reasons why one might decide to live downheartedly, from not knowing there's an alternative to loving the attention that despondency can bring. All the relatives gather around. You are the center of everyone's focus. They wonder, "What can we do to make you happy?"

Make no mistake. *You* are the only one who can make you happy. People can buy you fabulous presents and do all manner of nice things for you, but if you don't want to be cheered up, you won't be.

Once you have consciously decided you want to be happy, there are some great tools to help you bring more joy to your life. Achor lists seven principles and gives numerous strategies for creating happiness in his book, *The Happiness Advantage: The Seven Principles of Positive Psychology That Fuel Success and Performance at Work.*

Robert Holden, a leader in the development of positive psychology in the United Kingdom, has created an online course, *Happiness NOW! Timeless Wisdom for Feeling Good FAST.* It is filled with delightful stories, exercises, and poetry to inspire readers to get happy now.

As previously mentioned, other simple and effective tools for bringing joy into your life are The Passion Test and The Passion Test for Business, which Janet Bray Attwood and Chris Attwood present in their book, *The Passion Test: The Effortless*

Path to Discovering Your Life Purpose. They argue that your purpose is found in living a joyous, passion-filled life. To do this, you must first know what your passions are. They encourage you to list out ten to fifteen answers to the question, "When my life is ideal, I am…" or "When my work life is ideal, I am…" Then, they show you how to determine your top five priorities.

Once you know your highest passions, you can use them as a GPS to guide you in building a joy-filled life. They urge that, "Whenever you are faced with a choice, a decision, or an opportunity, choose in favor of your passions." This way, you will consistently make decisions that will make you happy, which will lead to you fulfilling your purpose—that is, your dharma.

The Attwoods' book instructs readers in how to identify goals and build action plans to support their passionate lives. An underlying strategy is to use the success formula, "intention, attention, no tension."

The first step in building your new life is to "intend" to do so—that is, to decide you are going to do it. Then, put your "attention" on all the steps that will help you realize your goal. Finally, because destiny is involved, you must accept that you cannot control all the events and synchronicities that occur. You have to let go, and adapt an attitude of "no tension." Struggling against the outcome of your efforts will lead to unhappiness. You need to believe that, on some level, the Universe knows what is best for you and can orchestrate events to achieve results beyond your imagining.

Of course, your Prarabdha Karma may also be involved (for better or for worse). In this case, your fate has been determined by your deeds in a past life, no matter your present activities.

The Upanishad, a sacred Hindu treatise, written 800–200 B.C., describes the relation between desire (passion), intention, and destiny in this way:

> You are what your deep, driving desire is.
> As your desire is, so is your will.
> As your will is, so is your deed.
> As your deed is, so is your destiny.
> *Brihadaranyaka Upanishad IV.4.5*

THE LAW OF ATTRACTION MEETS TOSHA SILVER

Do you consciously want to create a wildly positive destiny? Countless spiritual books promise that you can manifest anything you want by envisioning your desires in minute detail, keeping your vibration high—that is, thinking positively—and taking actions, no matter how small, in the direction of your dreams. Want three million dollars? You've got it. How about meeting your true soulmate? He is waiting for you to co-create him. Maybe it's the job opportunity of a lifetime you crave? Right around the corner.

Underlying all these promises is the authors' belief in the power of positive thinking and the Law of Attraction. Mike Dooley, a Hay House author, proclaims time and again, "Thoughts become things." It follows that if you want to create a joy-filled future, you need to think positive thoughts. Negative thoughts will just multiply the number of negative things in your life. The Law of Attraction—that is, like energy attracts like energy—commands this. Dwell in negativity and you'll attract more doom and gloom.

Tosha Silver, author of *Outrageous Openness: Letting the Divine Take the Lead* and *It's Not Your Money: How to Live Fully from Divine Abundance,* offers an alternative path. She does not dismiss the power of positive thinking or the Law of Attraction. She scoffs, however, at the notion of giving the Divine (God, Shakti, the Universe, whatever term you use to describe a higher power) a to-do list of what you'd like her to create. Instead, she urges you to give your desires to the Divine, trusting that she will create the perfect destiny for you. After all, the Divine knows the bigger picture and can manifest your goals in ways that never would have occurred to you.

Twice, the Divine has brought me wealth in ways I could not have imagined. The first time I was picked to be a director of First Deposit National Bank in the depressed northern town of Tilton, New Hampshire. I was eminently qualified to be on this board because I was well educated, was a certified financial planner, had actively worked on the community's small business and economic development initiatives, and I lived in the town's catchment area. I was paid a modest sum for my work.

However, through a series of events, First Deposit Bank became Providian National Bank, a wholly owned subsidiary of Providian Financial Corporation in San Francisco, California, which went public. My modest compensation skyrocketed as I was propelled into becoming a director of a subsidiary of a publicly traded company. My newfound finances supported my daughter's education and my exit from a dead marriage. Once her schooling was financed and I was safely divorced, the market crashed, and I was out of my director's job. Providian Financial Corporation was bought by Washington

Mutual Bank, which went bankrupt in the housing debacle. My Prarabdha Karma?

More recently, I wondered how I was going to support my retirement so that I could live well and give generously without worrying. I happened to look at the Zillow estimates for a condo I'd bought in 2013. To my astonishment, Zillow reported that my condo had appreciated more than 60 percent in value. Regardless of whether or not Zillow's estimates are reliable, it never occurred to me that my condo's appreciation might bring me retirement security. I am well aware that the housing market could tank tomorrow. Still, I take comfort in its position today.

I urge you to read Silver's books to learn more about creating abundance by letting the Divine lead the way. It may not be a quickly learned skill. Most of us have to diligently practice handing our worries over to the Divine. Know that if you do, your relief from anxiety will be profound. It is exhilarating to know that a power greater than you has your highest interest well in hand.

Never one to paint a totally rosy picture, though, I remind you that your best manifesting efforts may fall prey to your karma. If this is the case and the Divine is leading, rest assured that your fate is ultimately for the highest good of the universe and you.

DESTINY TALKS JOURNAL PROMPTS

1. What or who has brought you sustained happiness? Why?
2. Complete the sentence, "When my life is ideal, I am..."[2]

    List as many activities and circumstances as you'd like. Examples of answers might include: "I am connecting joyfully with friends and family." "I am living peacefully in a house overlooking the sea." "I am enjoying radiant health as I dance the night away." How can you make your present life more like the wonderful life you envision?

---

[2] Janet Bray Attwood and Chris Attwood. *The Passion Test: The Effortless Path to Discovering Your Life Purpose* (New York: Penguin Group, 2008), 30.

XI

GUIDING YOUR JOURNEY: NAVIGATIONAL TOOLS ENCORE

INTUITION AND THE CARDS

How does the Divine communicate with us? Through our sixth sense: our intuition.

In addition to using your passions as a GPS, you can use your intuition to build a fulfilling life. This is a practiced skill that comes much easier to some than to others. Once again, there are hundreds of psychics, mediums, and spiritual guides who will happily instruct you on how to enhance your intuition. In general, they will tell you that your intuition talks to you through your senses—that is, through:

> Clairaudience: You will hear the answer to your question.

Clairvoyance: You will receive a picture or sign telling you what you need to know.

Clairsentience: Your feelings will guide you.

Clairalience: Smells and scents will enhance your understanding of a situation.

Clairgustance: Insights will come to you through a taste in your mouth, even if you aren't eating anything. The taste might jar your memory about a certain person or event.

Claircognizance: This is when you don't know how you received your answer, but you just know the answer and its outcome.

Usually, people have a primary and secondary method through which they receive messages from the Divine. Often it is through clairvoyance, perhaps as a visual in a book or a sign on the back of a car, or clairaudience, perhaps hearing the lyrics to a song or overhearing words in a conversation that directly address your concerns.

Tosha Silver can't imagine living her life without using her senses to look for Divine signs. She says it would be like going into a dark room and choosing not to turn on the light.

Many believe that you will receive the Divine's answer in meditation. There is a saying among meditators that, "Prayer is you talking to God. Meditation is God talking to you." You may not receive your answer while you're meditating, but it will come to you later.

A popular method of going deeper into your understanding of a question is through the use of tarot, oracle, or angel cards. These cards aid a reader in understanding the concerns of the person seeking advice. The cards enhance the reader's intuition—that is, her ability to use her sixth sense to plumb the depths of the person asking the questions, and to receive messages about which the reader has no logical way of knowing.

Cards fall into two basic categories: tarot and oracle. Angel cards can be classified as either tarot or oracle cards.

Tarot cards follow a set pattern. Though tarot card decks were created in the mid-15th century, modern English decks are modeled after the Rider-Waite deck, created in 1910 and named for the cards' author and illustrator, respectively. They contain twenty-two major arcana (emblematic picture) cards that represent significant life events. The tower card, for example, refers to a major life upheaval, such as a divorce or bankruptcy. The sun card is a happier card, auguring a positive outcome to any current struggle.

Then there are the minor arcana cards, which illustrate more transitory life events. Similar to a regular deck of playing cards, the minor arcana are presented in four suits with fourteen cards per suit. Each suit contains a page, knight, queen, and king, as well as ten numerical cards. The suits depict the elements of fire, water, earth, and air. The Rider-Waite suits are wands (fire), cups (water), pentacles (earth), and swords (air).

In recent years, artists have designed tarot card decks with great license. There are vampire, angel, fairy, unicorn, Celtic, and witch tarot decks, to name a few. While the illustrations may have different themes, all traditional tarot decks have the same structure: twenty-two major arcana cards and fifty-six suit cards, for a total of seventy-eight cards.

Oracle cards, by contrast, are unique in their structure and illustrations. Colette Baron-Reid, for example, has created a sixty-eight-card deck infused with animal spirits, and another Goddess Power oracle deck with fifty-two cards.

The decks are *oracle* cards because, like traditional tarot, they can illuminate the present and predict the future. They do not contain, however, major or minor arcana cards or suits, nor do the cards represent life's journey in an orderly sequence.

A large subset of tarot and oracle cards is angel cards, which gained popularity through Doreen Virtue's work. Angel decks come with a varied number of cards and are often designed around a theme such as romance angels, archangels, healing angels, or life purpose cards. Once again, these cards are almost universal in their positive imagery. Doreen Virtue no longer promotes angel card readings, but Kyle Gray, a talented Scotsman bedecked with tattoos, has picked up her mantle and created Angel and Ancestors, Keepers of the Light, and Angel Prayer oracle cards.

Hybrid decks, such as the angel tarot deck created by Radleigh Valentine or the Akashic tarot deck developed by Sharon Anne Klingler and Sandra Anne Taylor, generally contain major and minor arcana. The cards' illustrations, nevertheless, are more positively drawn. Unlike traditional tarot decks, they do not contain death, hangman, or devil cards per se, so that questioners won't immediately jump to literal, frightening interpretations of the cards. While Valentine's angel tarot deck has the traditional seventy-eight cards, Klingler and Taylor's Akashic tarot deck contains only sixty-two cards.

Cards are highly symbolic. They provide a kind of Rorschach test where the reader can access the cards' meanings through her intuition. The reader may even ask the questioner what she sees in a card. If there's a door, for example, what lies behind its opening? Does it lead to a sunny path lined with daffodils and roses, or is the vista beyond it forbidding with threatening clouds? What indeed does the door represent? Is it a choice facing the questioner? And what alternative decisions do the two paths depict?

Tarot and oracle cards draw on the intuition of both the reader and the questioner. The reader's challenge is to interpret the cards as a projection of the questioner's psyche and fate. If the questioner fears the public spotlight, for example, opening a door that leads to fame and recognition may lead to a frightful landscape. However, at the end of the frightful path might gleam the Emerald City.

CREATIVE VISUALIZATION, VIBRATIONAL FREQUENCY, AND THE LAW OF ATTRACTION

More than forty years ago, Shakti Gawain, who died in 2018, published the seminal book, *Creative Visualization: Use the Power of Your Imagination to Create What You Want in Your Life*. She defined this process simply as "the technique of using your imagination to create what you want in your life." Today, New Age spiritualists almost universally proclaim creative visualization as a critical element in manifesting whatever you'd like in your life. If you can imagine already having what you seek, you will draw it into your future.

Before I started writing this book, I drew a cover for it as if it had already been published. My business coach at the time urged me to think of great crowds of people coming to hear me speak and wanting a signed copy. If nothing else, this is a pleasant fantasy that raises my spirits.

This brings me to another key concept in creating your destiny: raising your vibrational frequency. Esther Hicks and her now-deceased husband, Jerry Hicks, are largely responsible for popularizing this method of manifestation. Esther Hicks channels an entity she calls Abraham, who claims that emotions have vibrational frequencies. The more positive the emotion, the higher the frequency or energy it emits. At the low end of the scale are fear, grief, depression, despair, and powerlessness. At the high end are joy, knowledge, empowerment, freedom, love, and appreciation. In order to realize your desires, you must dwell in the higher vibrational emotions.

The Law of Attraction underlies this belief. It states that like energy attracts like energy. You cannot attract a positive event if you are emitting negative energy because your negativity will attract negative events.

Part of the success of creative visualization and The Passion Test lies in their raising your vibrational frequency. If you feel happy about what you are visualizing, your energy is likely to draw it to you. Similarly, if you use your passions to direct your course, your joy in doing this will create your success. Perhaps your joy is your success.

DESTINY TALKS JOURNAL PROMPTS

1. What are the primary and secondary ways that your intuition speaks to you? Hearing, sight, feelings, smell, taste, or a sense of just knowing?
2. When has your intuition revealed a truth or future event to you?
3. Are you willing to let your intuition guide your life? Why or why not?

XII

SKIRTING TREACHEROUS SHOALS, PART 1

Your demons lurk in darkness, ever ready to sabotage your trip. The worst among these are self-criticism and a lack of self-confidence. They can deep-six your best efforts.

If you are constantly criticizing yourself and you lack self-confidence, you might turn your ship around or, worse yet, abandon it altogether. Yet if you can build your confidence, your journey's success is almost assured. You will know abundant riches, a treasure chest filled with emeralds, rubies, sapphires, and diamonds.

There is no surefire way to accomplish this, but if you are committed to cherishing your very soul, there are lots of tools to aid in your endeavors. You will need to return to these tools time and again. Turning your ship around from low to high self-confidence is not for the faint-hearted. It takes dedication.

LIMITING BELIEFS

If you believe you cannot do or have something, then it follows, as night the day, that you will not do or have it. Sometimes though, you don't even know what the limiting beliefs are that prevent you from realizing your dreams. The work of speaker and author, Byron Katie, and the Austrian doctor and psychotherapist, Alfred Adler, can help you identify limiting beliefs and pry their grasping fingers off your back.

At the heart of both their methods is asking yourself if your negative beliefs are really true, and how do you know that they are true. If you don't know that they are true, then maybe they are false. Once you realize that your negative, limiting beliefs may be totally wrong, you can then choose more positive beliefs that will create a happier life for you going forward.

Byron Katie calls her line of inquiry The Work. It is aimed at eradicating "the thoughts that cause all suffering." It consists of four questions to ask yourself about any limiting belief:

1. Is it true? (Yes or no. If no, move to 3.)
2. Can you absolutely know that it's true? (Yes or no.)
3. How do you react, what happens, when you believe that thought?
4. Who would you be without the thought?

You can find out more about The Work and how to use it at Katie's website, www.thework.com.

While Byron Katie is a modern-day practitioner, Alfred Adler completed his work at the beginning of the 20th century. He is best known for his efforts to address inferiority complexes and his belief that societal forces interact with a person's interior feelings to determine his development.

Like many psychotherapists, he believed that people's self-concepts are almost entirely formed by the age of six or seven and that, as we grow older, we look for examples which confirm our opinion. Imagine how absurd and detrimental this can be—that we live our adult lives from the perspective of a young child.

As we sauntered home after clothes shopping, I complimented Jackie, who is in her sixties now, on her fashion sense. We were discussing our choice of careers. I asked Jackie why she hadn't pursued her love of fashion and her skill at choosing and buying clothes. She sighed. Then she told the story of how, when she was in the second grade, she loved to sketch women in fashionable clothes and how one of her classmates mocked her drawings. Jackie immediately stopped sketching and denied her interest in clothing. We fell silent as we contemplated that a second grader's uninformed taunts dissuaded Jackie from ever looking into a fashion-related career.

Many of us could match Jackie's story with how young classmates' and siblings' taunts made us think small.

Stories like these illustrate why it is so important to examine, once again, our childhood experiences. We should look for those passions which were thwarted. They contain rich insights for building an outstanding destiny. If you examine how and why you stopped pursuing a passion, you will gain insights into the consequences. You can then make a more well-informed decision about where you want to go in the future.

MONEY, MONEY, MONEY

Why is it that money plays such a debilitating role in keeping us from greatness? If you want to find where limiting beliefs hang out, just look at the role that money has played in your life. I wonder how many talented artists have abandoned ship because they did not want to starve. Whether or not they could have made money while enriching our culture with their genius is lost to history.

I have spent most of my life not following my desired career path, writing, because I didn't think I could earn a living at it. I may never succeed as a writer, but I would be so much better at this craft if I had honed it over the years.

The talented executive consultant, Beth Lefevre, has developed a three-day workshop, Money and Life Freedom, to guide participants in overcoming their limiting beliefs about money. One of her insightful exercises is built on Adler's work. She asks participants to write three stories describing their earliest memories about money. Once they have written these stories, they look for the lessons they learned in their youth and how these lessons have played out in their lives. Lefevre helps participants examine the truth of the lessons learned and if, and how, they can be transformed into positive lessons for personal growth.

One of the reasons that the Law of Attraction garners so many students is that many of us would like to bring more money into our lives by just thinking positive thoughts. We talk about wanting abundance, which is a fancy way of saying we want money, and more. First, we'd like the financial freedom and security that money buys, and then, we concede that money can't buy happiness, so we state that we'd really like abundance. No shame in this; it's human nature.

There are plenty of anecdotes about how visualizing, raising our vibrations, and the Law of Attraction have brought big bucks to those who have used them effectively. There are also plenty of stories about how folks just can't manifest the money they want to save their lives. Then there are those of us who make a living explaining why our clients' manifesting efforts have or have not worked. The reasons, of course, are ultimately unknowable.

As is her wont, Tosha Silver offers another perspective on bringing money into our lives. She argues that it isn't "our" money; it's the Divine's. By recognizing that money comes from the Divine—or the Source or whatever name you give it—you can get the money-focused stress monkey off your back. Since the Divine has an unlimited supply, the amount of wealth you have does not depend on you wresting it from someone else.

I've often thought how helpful this concept would be in divorce hearings. The parties would realize that, despite their wildest efforts, whatever is meant to come to them will, and whatever is not meant to come their way will be diverted.

How, you might wonder, could giving your money worries to the Divine alleviate stress when you still don't have the money you need, and you can't control how you will get it? This is the very point. You're not in control. You can take steps that are likely to bring money into your life, but you cannot know whether or not they will succeed. So, why not give up the worry and anxiety you attach to getting money, since it's ultimately out of your hands?

To give up trying to control where your money comes from requires a leap of faith. You need to believe that the Divine has your back. You should put your best effort into making money but understand that you cannot direct the outcome of your efforts. As Hamlet says, "There's a divinity that shapes our ends/Rough-hew them how we will." Divinity may direct you onto an alternative route to an amazing island that you didn't know existed. To do this, many of us will need to create a well of faith from which we can draw again and again.

Recently, I had an eye-opening and calming experience around money. It came through a consultation with Ellen Rogin, CPA and CFP®, a financial advisor with twenty years of experience. In addition to the traditional wealth-building services she offers, Rogin will talk to money on your behalf.

Before our conference, Ellen asked me some fundamental questions about my background. She then meditated and spoke to money about my situation. Money's insights confirmed my experiences. I know how to manage money but had left behind my positive relationship with money when I left my university job to set up my consulting and writing business. Still money was taking care of me behind the scenes. It was sending me "winks" by increasing the value of my assets and sending me other gifts. Money encouraged me to re-establish my relationship to it, to continue my present pursuits, and to know that I will be compensated for giving value, and that it will continue to send me "winks."

Somehow, I found this knowledge comforting. It rang true. The peace I experienced remains with me, weeks after my consultation. The consultation helped me come to terms with some of my own limiting beliefs about money.

Rogin and Lisa Kueng wrote the *New York Times* bestselling book, *Picture Your Prosperity: Smart Money Moves to Turn Your Vision into Reality*. It is the best book I've read on building wealth and financial security because it combines the inspirational with the practical. In the early chapters, they teach the reader how to identify her values and envision her picture of true prosperity. Later chapters give practical instruction, written in a highly readable style, on how to bring your prosperity picture to life. The authors also argue persuasively that gratitude and generosity are the keys to building wealth. They provide a roadmap for directing your money destiny. You can find out more about Rogin at her website, www.ellenrogin.com.

DESTINY TALKS JOURNAL PROMPTS

1. List all your limiting beliefs without editing. Then identify the top three to five beliefs that hold you back the most.

2. Can you identify where these beliefs came from? How old were you when you started believing each one?

3. What money beliefs influence your earning and spending patterns? For example, do you believe that money doesn't grow on trees or that rich people are greedy? What effects have these beliefs had on how much money you have and how you use it? Can you turn any of these beliefs around to your advantage?

XIII

SKIRTING TREACHEROUS SHOALS, PART 2

MORE ON CREATIVE VISUALIZATION

Signs and intuitive tools can instruct you on how to overcome limiting beliefs and realize your most cherished goals. Ask for assistance. Better yet, thank the Divine for the assistance she is already providing you. A critical step in visualization and other manifestation efforts is acting as if you already have what you seek.

One of the first advocates of this method was Florence Scovel Shinn, who wrote *The Game of Life and How to Play It* and *Your Word is Your Wand* in the 1920s. Countless others, including Shakti Gawain, Louise Hay, Wayne Dyer, and Tosha Silver, realized Shinn was onto something and have expanded on her work.

Shinn, a writer and illustrator, was one of the first spiritualists to articulate the Law of Attraction. She based her belief
on Christ's teaching that "Whatsoever a man soweth that shall
he also reap." She explains:

> This means that whatever man sends out in
> word or deed, will return to him; what he
> gives, he will receive.
>
> If he gives hate, he will receive hate; if he gives
> love, he will receive love; if he gives criticism,
> he will receive criticism; if he lies, he will be
> lied to; if he cheats, he will be cheated. We are
> taught also that the imaging faculty plays a
> leading part in the game of life...
>
> This means that what man images, sooner or
> later externalizes in his affairs.[3]

Shinn believed that you must understand your end goal
and state it as if you had already received it. In this way, you
will attract the result you desire. If, for example, you long to
be rich, you should thank the Divine for already granting
your wish, "Thank you, God, for providing me with all the
riches I need." If you would like guidance on how to increase
your wealth, you would thank the Divine for showing you
the next step you should take. If you want to know if you're
on the right path, you could say thank you to the Divine for
letting you know that you are on the right path. Underlying

---

[3]   Florence Scovel Shinn, *The Complete Works of Florence Scovel Shinn*,
(Mineola, New York: Dover Publications, Inc., 2010), 3.

your statements is the belief that the right path and outcome—which is for your highest good—have already been selected by the Divine.

Tosha Silver offers a wonderful "Change Me Prayer" for guidance:

> Please show me your Divine Will in this matter and send a clear sign that gives the proper direction. And if for some reason I'm about to head the wrong way, please, please stop me.[4]

Who knows where the sign with the answer to your question will appear? It could be on a store sign, the title of a book you glance at, a passage in an article you happen to read, or a lyric in a song that pops into your mind. Be on the lookout for it. This is your Divine guidance.

Napoleon Hill wrote one of the best-selling self-help books of all time, *Think and Grow Rich*, in 1937. It explains how to apply the power of positive thinking and the Law of Attraction to wealth creation. Positive thinking is only one of the arrows in Hill's quiver for growing rich. Inspired by Andrew Carnegie, Hill spent more than twenty years studying the methods by which the 100 wealthiest men in America in the early 20th century achieved their fortunes. These included self-made titans of industry and inventors extraordinaire: Henry Ford, J.P. Morgan, John D. Rockefeller, Alexander Graham Bell, and Thomas Edison.

---

[4]   Tosha Silver, *Outrageous Openness: Letting the Divine Take the Lead* (New York: Atria Books, 2014), 89.

Hill described their wealth-creating methods in sixteen laws for success and thirteen philosophic principles. Hill inspires his readers with such quotable aphorisms as:

> What the mind can conceive and believe it can achieve.

> You are the master of your destiny. You can influence, direct and control your environment. You can make your life what you want it to be.

To my mind, *Think and Grow Rich* goes far beyond prescriptions for how to make money. It's one of the best inspirational and practical guidebooks for creating the destiny of your choice.

A word of caution. Your road might not include a direct beeline, working 24/7, on your passion as riches multiply in your bank account. You could sink into debt and poverty as you work away. The Universe may signal that you need to nourish your talent as it grows from a seedling into a flowering plant.

Elizabeth Gilbert, author of *Eat, Pray, Love* and *Big Magic*, admonishes readers not to make their craft support their livelihood until it can easily do so. If you demand too much from your artistic endeavors, those endeavors may become onerous, no longer bringing you joy, but instead creating undue anxiety because they need time and nurturing before they can yield their fruit.

I know from coaching hundreds of entrepreneurs that you need to find the right time to start your venture. It is sometimes better to build your resources, skills, and contacts before cutting yourself loose from your moorings. However, if you follow intuition and Divine guidance, know that—as Christian Michelsen, a guru of personal coaches, likes to say—"Your success is inevitable." You may experience setbacks along the way, but in the end, if you consistently apply yourself toward your goals, you will succeed.

MAGIC MIRROR ON THE WALL, WHO'S THE FAIREST OF THEM ALL?

The mirror is supposed to give you the answer—right?! Not according to today's spiritualists. You tell the mirror the answer, and the mirror reflects the answer back to you. And woe be to you if you don't answer—nay, *believe*—that *you* are the fairest.

As previously mentioned, Louise Hay built a self-help/inspirational publishing empire advocating the healing effects of affirmations and mirror work. Hay House, the premier international publisher of New Age and spiritual books and online courses, grew out of Hay's belief in the healing powers of positive thoughts and self-love. She accomplished it all after the age of sixty. Louise Hay died in 2017 at age ninety.

Hay's work has helped millions of people. It can help you as well.

Hay's work emanated from her personal experiences. Louise Hay was raised by an abusive stepfather. She was raped by a neighbor when she was five years old. In her early fifties, she was diagnosed with "incurable" cervical cancer. At the time, she was a member of the First Church of Religious Science. She was heavily influenced by the writings of Florence Scovel Shinn, who believed in the power of positive thinking, and Ernest Holmes, who thought positive beliefs could cure bodily ills. Shinn's and Holmes's philosophies were built, in turn, on the unpublished works of Phineas Quimby, who preached in the 19th century.

Hay credited the practical application of these philosophies with curing her. Hay believed that if she could release her resentment about the abuse she had suffered, she would be healed. She followed a regimen of forgiveness, therapy, nutrition, reflexology, and occasional colonic enemas. Her cancer went into remission. Hay lived another forty years and spearheaded a spiritual empire that has inspired millions of people to create healthier, more fulfilled lives.

In 1984, Louise Hay self-published *You Can Heal Your Life*, which chronicles how to heal specific ailments with specific affirmations. Affirmations are merely positive statements such as, "I have the self-esteem, power, and confidence to move forward in life with ease."

More than fifty million copies of Hay's book have been sold. It has been published in thirty languages.

In the 1980s, Hay also began mirror work with AIDS patients. She initially drew together five or so patients, but soon ended up running sessions with thousands of sufferers. She urged patients to use a mirror to stare deep into their eyes, down into their souls, and say, "I love you. I truly love you." Other affirmations included, "I choose to feel good about myself," "I am worthy of love," and "I am willing to let life love me totally."

The mirror work helped heal the patients' wounded souls by ending their self-criticism.

At the time, society shunned AIDS patients. People were irrationally afraid of catching AIDS from even casual contact from sufferers. The disease also condemned its victims to horrible suffering, exorbitantly expensive treatments that few could afford, and certain death. One cannot imagine the mental anguish that societal condemnation and the inability to control one's fate heaped onto the physical torture that AIDS patients experienced.

Louise Hay taught self-love as a way to control one's fate. Her students, who were gulping seawater in a deep, lonely, and tumultuous ocean of pain, must have felt that a lifeboat had suddenly come upon them.

No matter what ailment or distress you suffer, you can use affirmations and mirror work to build your self-esteem and, *perhaps*, to cure your disease. It doesn't cost anything to do, but takes self-discipline, especially if you have hounded yourself with negative self-talk over the years. You will need to change the negativity into positivity.

Hay House now has hundreds of authors spread out across the world whose writings, courses, and workshops can help you accomplish this. Louise Hay's most recent work is contained in *Loving Yourself: Online Video Course* and *Life Loves You: 7 Spiritual Practices to Heal Your Life*, co-authored with Robert Holden.

As previously mentioned, Esther Hicks, channeling the nonphysical entity Abraham, underlines the importance of the self-love that forms the basis of Hay's teachings. In a workshop given on May 30th, 2000, Abraham relayed the message:

> Appreciation and self-love are the most important tools that you could ever nurture. Appreciation of others, and the appreciation of yourself, are the closest match to your Source Energy of anything that we've ever witnessed anywhere in the universe.

Emotional Freedom Technique

The Emotional Freedom Technique, commonly referred to as EFT or just "tapping," is another proven strategy for alleviating stress and enhancing good health. It combines meditation with tapping on meridians, which, according to Chinese medicine, are pathways in the body along which vital energy flows. Nick Ortner and Mark Hyman's book, *The Tapping Solution: A Revolutionary System for Stress-Free Living,* explains how it works.

The person seeking relief taps along a sequence of meridians while describing the pain he is suffering. Eventually the description of the pain gives way to more positive statements about resolving the problem. This is a simplistic explanation of the process. If you are interested in EFT, there's a wealth of information about it on the internet. Ortner produced *The Tapping Solution* documentary film to show how it works and to popularize the method. The documentary features experts and patients using the technique to miraculously heal lifelong illnesses that had resisted other medical regimens.

EFT has gained worldwide recognition as an effective treatment for emotional, psychological, and physical ailments. Researchers from Harvard Medical School and other institutions have demonstrated how and why tapping works. You may want to add EFT to your tools for navigating rough waters on your life journey.

Note that neither Louise Hay nor Nick Ortner are doctors. You should consult a trained health or mental health care professional before embarking on a course of treatment for an ailment.

DESTINY TALKS JOURNAL PROMPTS

1. At this point, you should have some idea about what lights you up and what you long to accomplish in this life. What is holding you back from living a passionate life and realizing your dreams?

2. Which modalities—creative visualization, affirmations, mirror work, and/or EFT—can you use to counteract your doubts? Are there other ways you can increase your self-confidence?

XIV

THE ELECTRICITY TO JUICE YOUR NAVIGATIONAL TOOLS

You'll need to plug into faith, detachment, gratitude, and joy to realize your chosen destiny.

FAITH AND DETACHMENT

I touched on faith's vital role in the section on overcoming limiting beliefs about money. Let me reiterate the importance of faith.

The tools you select may yield immediate results. It's just as likely that the delayed arrival of tangible, material manifestations of your desires will try your patience. As with religion, spiritual beliefs require a considerable dose of faith. Each of the modalities that I've explained have their adherents and empirical data to demonstrate that they work. Nevertheless, no one claims that they work for everyone in the same way. It's the height of frustration to hear how someone has achieved peace of mind through mirror work and affirmations, for example, while you remain mired in negative self-doubt.

Hand in hand with faith, detachment to the outcome of your efforts will alleviate your stress. I first read about detachment in Deepak Chopra's bestseller, *The Seven Spiritual Laws of Success,* published in 1994. Detachment is a hard concept to embrace if you are intensely visualizing what you want and madly taking steps to make it happen. Remember the formula: intention, attention, no tension. This urges you to first set an intention about what you'd like to achieve. Then you should focus all your energy—your attention—on realizing your goal. Once you have put your best effort forward, you need to relax—have no tension—about what the outcome of your efforts will be.

This takes you back to faith. You need to believe that whatever outcome your striving leads to, it is for your highest good. To achieve peace of mind in this process, you need to believe that there is a benign universal force that has your best interest in hand.

As Deepak Chopra eloquently explains:

> In detachment lies the wisdom of
> uncertainty...
> In the wisdom of uncertainty lies the freedom
> From our past, from the known,
> Which is the prison of past conditioning.

> And in our willingness to step into the
> Unknown, the field of all possibilities,
> We surrender ourselves to the creative mind
> that orchestrates the dance of the universe.[5]

If we cling to our desired outcome, we are clinging to the certainty of what our past has taught us to expect. We limit the possibilities for realizing a more creative outcome that we cannot imagine but which the Universe can design. Some spiritualists recommend that you write, "This or something better," after listing your goals to recognize the role of the Divine.

You can sabotage your intentions by focusing too doggedly on what you want. Sandra Anne Taylor calls this "paradoxical intent." If you feel desperate to bring in more money or find your soulmate, for example, the harshness of the desperate energy you generate will push the money and perfect love away. Your intention, because of the essentially negative energy which fuels it, will paradoxically push away the very thing you want to manifest.

I have experienced this. When I am enthusiastic and easy about achieving a goal, the path to success unfolds effortlessly. I remember when I was interviewing for a bank job, but secretly thinking that I really wanted to be on the bank's board. I casually mentioned this desire to a champion of mine at the bank. Before two months had passed, due to synchronistic events, I was a director on the bank's board.

In contrast, when I first went out on my own, I pushed hard on the gas pedal. I said countless affirmations and visualized clients beating down my door, but my money well

---

[5]   Deepak Chopra, *The Seven Spiritual Laws of Success: A Practical Guide to the Fulfillment of Your Dreams* (San Rafael, CA: Amber-Allen Publishing and New Word Library, 1994), 81.

had dried up. Finally, I thought, *It doesn't matter what I'm doing. The Divine will take care of me.* The proverbial floodgates opened up. Money appeared in unanticipated ways.

Buddhism teaches that attachment is the root of all suffering. You only suffer to the extent that you care whether or not your plans lead to a specific result. If you aren't attached to the means of achieving an outcome nor to the outcome itself, but enjoy the journey, you can happily accept what shows up. You don't have to worry about the process. It will all work out.

In the 2011 movie, *The Best Exotic Marigold Hotel,* the Indian manager comforts his frazzled, elderly British guests, by saying, "Everything will be okay in the end. If it's not okay, it's not the end."

GRATITUDE

Gratitude is your ultimate armor against downheartedness, limiting beliefs, and losing faith in your ability to attain your goals. Feeling gratitude raises your spirits.

If you are feeling particularly depressed, you may wonder what you can be grateful for. There is always something to be grateful for.

Look around you. Is the sun shining? Do you have comfortable clothes? Do you anticipate eating well? Is there someone you care for or who cares for you? Is there a song that brings you joy? The possibilities are endless. The minute you focus your attention on what you appreciate now, you will begin to increase your vibrational energy and realize more things that you are grateful for.

As the saying goes, "What you appreciate, appreciates." It increases in amount and in value.

Once you have turned your downward spiral into an upward spiral, you will surely be on the path to spiritual abundance. You can't feel down while you are actively acknowledging all the riches in your world.

By practicing gratitude every day, you tap into your soul's essence and learn what constitutes your bliss. You can then express your unique qualities as you seek out activities and people that spark your gratitude. Gratitude builds upon itself. The more grateful you feel, the more gratitude you create for yourself. If you follow this path, you will build a destiny that lights up your world.

"OH JOY! OH RAPTURE UNFORESEEN!"

A common denominator among all the spiritualists that I've quoted is their belief in the power of uplifting emotions: happiness, joy, bliss. The delight you seek must precede the life you create.

Focusing on the emotion you want to feel is more important than focusing on your goal. Happiness, as Shawn Achor so eloquently argues, creates success. You may experience happiness as a result of successfully achieving a goal, but it's a harder road to travel.

As previously pointed out, upon reaching the pinnacle of a metaphorical mountain, many comment, "Is this all there is?" They thought it would bring them happiness, but the joy is short-lived, and they realize they need another mountain to climb.

However, if they experience joy *while* climbing up the mountain, that joy is their companion. It will be with them on their descent. They can always access that bliss, whether or not they are climbing mountains, receiving medals, or basking in applause.

DESTINY TALKS JOURNAL PROMPTS

1. Do you believe that you can create a fabulous destiny? What events have shown you that the Universe/Divine values your soul's desires?
2. Are you attached to how your destiny manifests? Why or why not?
3. List people and things that you are grateful for. Include activities and people that make you smile. Whenever you are downhearted, return to this list. Are there things you could do, or people you could call, to raise your spirits?

XV

LET YOUR SOUL AND SPIRIT DIRECT YOUR DESTINY

At a bare minimum, you control 50 percent of your destiny. Your genes do not determine your fate, nor do haphazard events. They may influence the journey, but, rest assured, *you* are in charge. Research in epigenetics shows that the shape of a gene is influenced by the gene's environment, including a person's beliefs about his situation. This implies that you are not at the mercy of your heredity because, by altering your beliefs, you can determine the environment surrounding your genes.

Bruce Lipton, PhD, a leader in the field of epigenetics, reports that flawed genes cause less than 1 percent of all diseases. The most common cause of disease is stress. According to Lipton, 75 to 90 percent of all visits to a physician are for stress-related ailments. If you can manage the stress in your life, you can control how much time you spend in a doctor's office.

Similarly, only 50 percent of your happiness is determined by the happiness set point you were born with. The set point is the level of happiness that you return to when all other variables are held constant. You control your attitude, outlook, and other determinants of your happiness.

Some cataclysmic event, illness, or an amazing piece of good luck may befall you. Surely these events influence your course. They do, but *you* choose how you will react to the events. Your reaction will put into play a whole new series of events, which may be unknowable, but can yield gems if you look for them—not only for you, but for all earthly inhabitants.

One need only think of the many movements that have sprung from tragedies to know that this is true. Black Lives Matter, Mothers Against Drunk Driving, and the students from Parkland, Florida, who lobby against gun violence, spring to mind. These movements have resulted in altered laws which have curbed destructive behavior. They have saved thousands of lives. I would guess that their leaders, while they have suffered terrible grief, have channeled their grief into richly rewarding destinies.

Countless campaigns against debilitating illnesses spearheaded by sufferers, relatives, friends, and advocates have led to the near eradication of such diseases as smallpox and polio. I never could have imagined that there would be a cure for AIDS in my lifetime, but we are on the brink of developing one. ACT UP protesters spurred the demand for immediate research into finding an AIDS cure when the U.S. government's response was lackluster. The research is now yielding results.

None of these behavioral changes and cures would have been possible if someone had not believed she could influence destiny. Progress depends on the belief that humans can change the course of history. As George Bernard Shaw wrote in *Man and Superman*:

> The reasonable man adapts himself to the world; the unreasonable one persists in trying to adapt the world to himself. Therefore, all progress depends on the unreasonable man.

The first step in choosing your destiny is picking a destination—your Ithaka. Perhaps you've set your sights on a certain profession—becoming a doctor, actor, writer, or environmentalist, for example. Or maybe you don't know what you want to be, but you know what cause inspires you. You want to end poverty, combat climate change, or design awesome buildings.

The specific goal or destination you choose is only marginally important. You may change goals. Your initial destination may not be as rewarding as you thought it would be. How many of us have intensely run after a goal only to find a feeling of emptiness once the goal was achieved?

Not your destination, but your soul and spirit hold your destiny. Your soul is your essence, your light. It determines what brings you joy and fulfillment. If you let your soul be your rudder, you can use it to steer you to the perfect destination.

Your soul runs deep. It may seem too complex to understand, but coming to know it is infinitely rewarding. That is why there are so many tools to plumb its depths. From learning to read the stars and oracle cards to journaling and engaging in soul conversations, you can begin to know some of your soul's facets. Once you have discovered one facet, it will let you peer into innumerable prisms of sparkling lights.

Your spirit is the wind in your sails. If it is energized, your sails will billow. You will sail swiftly in your chosen direction.

If it is dejected, you will drift listlessly, perhaps even sink, as oncoming storms batter your ship.

It is imperative that you honor your soul and spirit. Treat them as the Divine gifts they are. As you start out on your journey, you need only have faith that they are the guides to your enlightened destiny and, indeed, to this planet's future.

Take the time and use the tools to understand them, then choose how you want to view your journey. Is the trip filled with the joy of discovery backed by a divine source, or is it one that bemoans a fate foisted upon it by negative, purposeless events? Your destiny, enlightened or a drudge, depends on this choice.

Our planet's future also depends on this choice. I am writing this in 2020. A darkness is shadowing our planet. A ferocious pandemic is laying waste to people's lives and the world economy. It's a frightening time. White supremacy and terrorist movements are rising. Authoritarian dictators are taking over the leadership of major countries, wielding their power with a vengeance and tenaciously holding on to their positions despite the will of their countries' people.

Let us not be a world where, in the words of the poet W.B. Yeats, "The best lack all conviction, while the worst are full of passionate intensity." We need to create a positive environment to overcome evil's influence. We do this by choosing every day to know and love ourselves. If you love yourself, you will not need to put anyone else down. Rather you will realize the power, indeed the delight, that comes from brightening another's day.

Your good thoughts will result in good actions. Their goodness will be like life's lake. It doesn't matter how small your pebble is. If millions of other people are throwing positive pebbles and stones into the lake, soon the lake will be filled with waves of goodness. In destiny language, we will all be creating oceans of good karma.

Unleash the power of your soul and spirit. Grab your ship's rudder, let out your sails to catch the wind. Determine your course. Gather your mates to enliven and safeguard your journey. Set sail!

DESTINY TALKS JOURNAL PROMPTS

1. Reread *Ithaka*, the poem by Constantine Cavafy, at the beginning of this book. What does it mean to you now? How far have you traveled?
2. Review your answers to the questions in previous chapters. What are your most significant insights?
3. Describe the destiny you would like to create. How can you make the journey to your destination joyful? Will you treasure its riches?

Bibliography

Adrienne, Carol. *The Numerology Kit*. New York: Plume, 1988.

Anchor, Shawn. *The Happiness Advantage: The Seven Principles of Positive Psychology that Fuel Success and Performance at Work*. New York: Crown Publishing Group, 2010.

Attwood, Janet Bray and Chris Attwood. *The Passion Test: The Effortless Path to Discovering Your Life Purpose*. New York: Penguin Group, 2008.

Benway, Katie. *Ignite Your Intrepid Soul: A Courageous Home for Your Human Heart*. Kindle Direct Publishing, 2020.

Bolt, Chandler. *Published. The Proven Path from Blank Page to Published Author*. Kindle Direct Publishing, 2016.

Buchanan, Michelle. *The Numerology Guidebook: Uncover Your Destiny and the Blueprint Of Your Life*. Carlsbad, CA: Hay House, Inc., 2013.

Cavafy, C.P. *Collected Poems, Revised Edition*, translated by Edmund Keeley and Philip Sherrard, edited by George Savidis, Princeton: Princeton University Press, Translation Copyright 1975, 1992.

Chopra, Deepak. *The Seven Spiritual Laws of Success: A Practical Guide to the Fulfillment Of Your Dreams*. San Rafael, CA: Amber-Allen Publishing & New World Library, 1994.

Cameron, Julia. *The Artist's Way: A Spiritual Path to Higher Creativity.* New York: Tarcherperigee, 2016.

Dispensa, Joe. *Becoming Supernatural: How Common People are Doing the Uncommon.* Carlsbad, CA: Hay House, 2017.

Gawain, Shakti. *Creative Visualization: Use the Power of Your Imagination to Create What You Want in Your Life.* Novato, CA: Nataraj Publishing, 1978.

Gerwick-Brodeur and Lisa Lenard. *The Complete Idiot's Guide to Astrology.* New York: Alpha Books, 2007.

Gibran, Kahlil. *The Prophet.* New York: Alfred A. Knopf, 1923.

Gilbert, Elizabeth. *Big Magic: Creative Living Beyond Fear.* New York: Riverhead Books, 2015.

Gray, Kyle. *Angel Numbers: The Message and Meaning behind 11:11 and other Number Sequences.* Carlsbad, CA: Hay House, Inc., 2019.

_____. *Light Warrior: Connecting with the Spiritual Power of Fierce Love.* Carlsbad, CA: Hay House, Inc., 2007.

Gregory, Alyse. *She Shall Have Music.* Sherborne, England: The Sundial Press, 2019.

_____. *The Cry of a Gull: Journals 1923-1948.* Edited by Michael Adam. Somerset, England: Out of the Ark Press, 1973.

Halvorson, Christine. *Inmate.* Kindle Direct Publishing, 2019.

_____. *Spinning Gold: A Workbook for Shaping Your Family Stories into Compelling Stories.* Kindle Direct Publishing, 2020.

Hay, Louise and Robert Holden. *Life Loves You: 7 Spiritual Practices to Heal Your Life.* Carlsbad, CA: Hay House, Inc., 2015.

Hill, Napoleon. *Think and Grow Rich! The Original Version Restored and Revised.* Aventine Press, 2008.

Holden, Robert. *Authentic Success: Essential Lessons and Practices from the World's Leading Coaching Program on Success Intelligence.* Carlsbad, CA: Hay House, Inc., 2011.

Jordan, Juno. *Numerology: The Romance in Your Name.* Camarillo, CA: Devorss & Company, 1965.

Lagerquist, Kay and Lisa Lenard. *The Idiot's Guide to Numerology.* New York: Alpha, 2004.

Lama, Dalai. *The Art of Happiness: A Handbook for Living.* New York: Riverhead Books, 2009.

Lama, Dalai and Desmond Tutu with Douglas Abrams. *The Book of Joy: Lasting Happiness in a Changing World.* New York: Avery, 2016.

Ortner, Nick and Mark Hyman. *The Tapping Solution: A Revolutionary System for Stress-Free Living.* Carlsbad, CA: Hay House, Inc., 2013.

Quigley, Patrick. *Sisters Against the Empire: Countess Constance Markievicz and Eva Gore Booth, 1916-1917.* Dublin: The Liffey Press, 2016.

Reeve, Christopher. *Still Me.* New York: Ballantine Books, 1998.

Rogin, Ellen and Lisa Kueng. *Picture Your Prosperity: Smart Money Moves to Turn Your Vision into Reality.* New York: Penguin Group, 2015.

Shinn, Florence Scovel. *The Complete Works of Florence Scovel Shinn.* Mineola, New York: Dover Publications, Inc., 2010.

Silver, Tosha. *It's Not Your Money: How to Live Fully from Divine Abundance.* Carlsbad, CA: Hay House, Inc., 2019.

_____. *Outrageous Openness: Letting the Divine Take the Lead.* New York: Atria, 2014.

Silverman, Debra. *The Missing Element: Inspiring Compassion for the Human Condition.* Rochester, VT: Findhorn Press, 2016.

Spiller. Jan. *Astrology for the Soul.* New York: Bantam Dell, 1997.

Taylor, Sandra Anne. *Quantum Success: The Astounding Science of Wealth and Happiness.* Carlsbad, CA: Hay House, Inc., 2006.

Weiss, Brian, M.D. *Many Lives, Many Masters: The True Story of a Prominent Psychiatrist, his Young Patient, and the Past-Life Therapy that Changed both their Lives.* New York: Simon & Schuster, 1988.

GLOSSARY

I'd like to clarify the terms that are sometimes employed interchangeably when discussing destiny. These include destiny, dharma, fate, free will, and karma. Scholars often disagree on the nuances between different words. I will define how I use the terms in this book.

DESTINY

Your destiny is your life events. It is the arc of your life—that is, the total of all that happens to you during your lifetime. It often has a positive connotation. People talk about destiny when a person has achieved something great—for example, created an inspiring work of art, amassed a fortune, devised a groundbreaking invention, built an international business, proposed a revolutionizing theory, or led a mass movement. Think Pablo Picasso, Madame Curie, Bill Gates, Henry Ford, Maya Angelou, Albert Einstein, Mahatma Gandhi, Martin Luther King, Jr., and Mother Teresa.

We look for signs of these individuals' genius in their youth. Then we can say with conviction, "They were destined for greatness. It was in their stars." They were born with the personal traits of a leader. When faced with challenges, their character determined that they would surmount adversity.

Inherent in the idea of destiny, as I and others employ it, is the belief that you can, to a certain extent, shape it. You can determine how you will react to events. If a horrific accident befalls you, you can choose whether or not to decline into despair or use your misfortune to create a larger destiny.

Christopher Reeve, the actor ironically known for his role as Superman, is an excellent example. Born in 1952, Reeve was a phenomenally talented and successful actor, extraordinarily handsome, and a gifted athlete. He appeared to have it all. On May 27, 1995, at age forty-three, he was competing in an equestrian event in Culpeper, Virginia. His horse balked at jumping the third fence, and Reeve was thrown to a new destiny. His first and second cervical vertebrae were crushed, his skull detached from his spine, and he couldn't breathe on his own. Reeve became a quadriplegic. He never regained the use of his arms and legs, nor was he ever able to breathe on his own again.

For the remaining nine years of his life, Reeve defied depression and deathly illnesses. During this time, he also became a world-renowned philanthropist and activist, championing the cause of patients with spinal cord injuries and advocating for stem cell research. He continued directing and acting. He directed the HBO film *In the Gloaming*, which won four CableACE Awards and was nominated for five Emmy Awards. His subsequent performance in *Rear Window* was nominated for a Golden Globe and won a Screen Actors Guild Award. Reeve also became a *New York Times* bestselling author with the publication of his autobiography, *Still Me*. Whether or not Reeve was born with the talent, perseverance, good looks, and fortune to continually rise to greatness is anyone's guess. Regardless, Christopher Reeve chose a Superman's destiny.

DESTINATION

The definitions of destination and destiny are distinct, yet the words are closely aligned. You set a destination, a place you are going to in the physical world. You can plan and be almost assured of reaching your destination. Destiny, on the other hand, has a metaphysical connotation. It's where you're headed in terms of your life, and while it may include a physical location, it generally refers to your life experiences. You can only control your destiny to a certain extent. Forces beyond your knowing often direct the turn of events in your life.

DHARMA

There is no direct English translation for the word, "dharma." Various Indian religions, including Buddhism, Hinduism, Jainism, and Sikhism, attribute different meanings to the concept of dharma. Loosely defined, it is the moral force that orders the universe.

Deepak Chopra, the renowned spiritual leader, interprets dharma as "purpose in life." In his book, *The Seven Spiritual Laws of Success: A Practical Guide to the Fulfillment of Your Dreams,* he argues that there are three underlying tenets to dharma. To paraphrase, he believes that:

1. Each of us is unique. We are here to discover our distinct gifts and talents.

2. We are also here to express our unique talent. He believes that everyone has one, maybe several, exceptional skills. When we use these skills, we become lost in time and are pursuing our dharma.

3. We need to use our unique talents to serve humanity. When we do this, we are living our dharma, our purpose in life.[6]

According to Chopra's definition, by discovering and living our dharma, we will realize our highest destiny and advance the interests of the universe. This fundamental belief underpins the teachings of *Destiny Talks.*

FATE

Destiny and fate are often considered synonyms—interchangeable words with the same meaning. However, they vary slightly in use. Destiny has more positive undertones. As already pointed out, it also indicates a certain level of human control. High achievers, like Oprah, talk about their destiny and personal legacy, not about their careers and fate.

Fate, in contrast, has a hard, immutable quality about it. Your fate is contained in the life events, diseases, fires, floods, accidents, meetings, and relationships that you never saw coming. You didn't seek them. Common statements include, "They were fated to meet each other," and "As fate would have it…" You could substitute destiny for fate in these phrases, but fate, with its sense that a larger force is directing the course of events, seems more appropriate.

---

[6]   *The Seven Spiritual Laws of Success,* 97-99.

FREE WILL

This book is all about free will. It's about taking the circumstances that are given to you and molding them into the future of your choice.

Free will is the opposite of fate. While greater, unknowable forces control your fate, *you* are in charge of your free will. Your will is what you choose to do or not do. It's free because no one else controls it. By exercising your free will, you can partially control your destiny.

We cannot know how many of our life events are predetermined and how many are determined by us. There's a continuum of belief. On one end is the belief that a universal force or entity controls all earthly events; on the other end is the belief that humans are totally in charge of events in their lives.

I believe that 25 to 50 percent of our circumstances are predetermined. The more I study metaphysics, the more I believe we create our own destinies. As described beforehand, epigenetic research demonstrates that our beliefs can change the environment in which our genes operate. This means that we can influence how the very genes that we were born with will operate.

Moreover, I believe that we cannot always control what befalls us, but we can determine how we react to life events. This is our free will—our power to create our destiny.

KARMA

Karma is about cause and effect. Whatever you put out will return to you in kind. If you act with positive intent and help others, you are creating "good karma." You will be rewarded with positive life experiences. On the other hand, if you seek to harm and are vengeful, you will eventually be smacked down.

The boomerang effect of your actions, good or evil, are not necessarily realized in your present lifetime. This is why you may hear someone say, "I must have done something good in a past life, because I'm so fortunate in this one."

Karma means "action" or "doing" in Sanskrit. The concept that your actions in this life will determine the kind and quality of your next life is a deeply spiritual subject which is explored extensively in various Buddhist sects with more subtlety than is presented here.

Your karma plays a strong role in determining your destiny, but it is not your destiny per se. Your actions have consequences for your life. Nevertheless, destiny and fate connote that larger, unknowable forces, in addition to your actions, determine your fortunes. In other words, karma is based on your actions, while destiny and fate are, to some degree, predetermined by unknown forces.

PRARABDHA KARMA

Prarabdha Karma, like destiny and fate, embraces the idea that larger, unknown forces direct your life. It posits that these forces dictate a curriculum of lessons for the higher good that each soul has come to earth to learn. Part of the joy of self-discovery is mastering these lessons.

ACKNOWLEDGEMENTS

My heartfelt thanks to:

Chris Halvorson for inspiring me to take my writing from journal entries to the published page, for editing my draft, and most of all, for being a dear friend,

Gina Calvano, my writing buddy, for sharing the highs and lows of writing and our lives, for helping me with my title, and for critiquing my book,

My inspiring guides: Katie Benway, Kyle Gray, Allice Haidden, and Beth Lefevre,

My extraordinary earth angels: Trine Kolding and Karen-Lynn Siperstein,

My fabulous clients, who are my students and my teachers,

Qat Wanders, CEO of Wandering Words Media, and her team, for their wise guidance in editing and publishing *Destiny Talks,*

Nanette Perrotte for her nourishing soul, outstanding talent, and enthusiasm for bringing my book to life on audio,

Kerk Murray, my fantastic coach, and the staff of Self-Publishing School, led by Chandler Bolt, who provided the curriculum to help me realize the dream of becoming an author,

My wonderful family, including sisters, brothers, sisters-in-law, nieces, nephews, an aunt, cousins, stepsons, and other members of an extraordinary soul group,

My friends: Molly McGregor Brandt, Jewel Fox, Sally Helms, Kit McCormick, Andrea O'Brien, Katharine Ogden Michaels, Deborah Osgood, and Anne Whitman, for providing invaluable support, insights, and laughter over the years,

Henry Kitchen for his enduring love and support, and

Jannie Kitchen for her wisdom, infectious laughter, steadfastness, generosity, and considerable editing skills.

ABOUT THE AUTHOR

 Janice Gregory co-authored the best-selling book, *The Happiness Code: How Small Habits Will Change Your Life Starting Today.* Her work is also featured in *The Powys Journal* in England. A certified coach, she is a numerologist, a Passion Test facilitator, and an oracle card reader. Prior to starting her coaching business, Janice was a small business consultant for twenty-five years with the University System of New Hampshire, where she designed award-winning, nationally recognized entrepreneurial programs. She earned her B.A. from Harvard College and her M.P.A. from the Harvard Kennedy School. Janice lives in Newburyport, Massachusetts and can be reached at www.janicegregory.com.

Connect to Your Purpose

Create Your Destiny Profile

In

Find Your Purpose: The Destiny Talks Workbook

Available at Amazon.com

Also, look for *Legacy Talks,* which explores the many ways to leave inspiring gifts in your lifetime. Sign up at www.janicegregory.com to be notified when *Legacy Talks* and other books become available.

Thank you for reading my book!

I really appreciate all your feedback, and I love hearing what you have to say.

I need your input to make my future books better.

Please leave an honest review on Amazon to let me know what you thought of *Destiny Talks*.

Thanks so much!

Janice Gregory

୯ᵌ May Your Destiny Shine Brightly
Like Your Extraordinary Soul!

Made in United States
North Haven, CT
11 June 2022

20122594R00085